BORN TO BELIEVE:

With Passion To Achieve
All God's Destined For Me

KAREN A. DESJARDINS

With love
to you Anita!
K Desjardins
Apr. 24/17

ISBN:-10: 1544148526
ISBN-13: 978-1544148526

DEDICATION

This book is dedicated to my mother, Lucille Blanche Desjardins and my brother, Michael Gerard Desjardins (known as Mike), who are now gone home to be with Jesus. I also dedicate this book to my loving family, my cousin Debbie Mantha and my dear friend Pamela John. They have been true living examples of Christ's everlasting love. I am truly grateful for their support and encouragement throughout my life. I hold a special place in my heart and prayers for each and every one of them.

Mom

Me and brother, Mike

ACKNOWLEDGMENTS

I would like to express my gratitude to all who allowed the mention of their names and sharing of some personal experiences.

I extend a special thank you to Debbie Mantha for allowing me to share some intimate details of her life experiences and her beautiful poem.

For my family's ongoing love, support and encouragement throughout the years, I am forever grateful. Each one of them has personally contributed to who I am today.

I give ultimate thanks to God for His many blessings throughout each and every year. Through His love and presence in my life, I was able to write this book and give honour and glory directly where it should be - to our loving and faithful FATHER, to JESUS CHRIST - our Lord and Saviour and to the HOLY SPIRIT.

CONTENTS

CHAPTER 1

INTRODUCTION

Writing poetry has helped me to express my thoughts and appreciation of life's challenges and rewards. As often mentioned throughout my life, both verbally and written, I give ultimate thanks to God up above who has made me complete with so many gifts of love.

I began writing poetry when I was in my teens and started up again in 1999, at which time I wanted to write a memorial poem in honour of my mother, Lucille Desjardins. I then decided to continue writing poetry as a way of journaling and expressing my innermost thoughts and experiences about life, love and faith. Through poetry writing, I can express my gratitude to God for where I am and who I am today.

In my hunger to serve and honour God, I have chosen to write this book to share of His tremendous love, His many blessings, and His promises for all believers as expressed in His Word. In doing so, I have included some of my poetry, insights, visions and personal testimonies.

By sharing my memoir and spiritual journey, I hope to inspire others who may have lost their way back to God, or to help those who as of yet, have not experienced such an intense love acquired through a personal relationship with God.

From my early childhood, my mother's determination in keeping God as our utmost priority in life has provided a deep trust in my faith, myself and in whatever life challenges come my way. Her love and dedication, as a wife and mother, forever lives on in our hearts ans in our actions and beliefs todays.

Karen, Mom, Brother (Mike),   Pat, Dad, Me (Karen)
Sister (Pat)

CHAPTER 2

BLINDED SIGHT

When we get caught up in our busy schedules and life circumstances, we often don't take time to stop and focus on God and His Word. We can get so trapped in worldly fears, guilt, doubt, jealousy and a whole range of negative thoughts and feelings that we tend to get blinded. By relying on our own abilities to rise above the negative and destructive situations around us, we end up blocking or limiting God's will for our life.

When we are oppressed by anxieties, fears, or any other uncertainties in our life that keep us mentally paralyzed and in bondage, we need to seek God for answers. We need to clear our hearts and minds and ask God to come in and speak to us. God always answers our prayers. If we still ourselves to everything else around us, we will hear Him speak to us and He will rescue us from our distress.

"The righteous cry out, and the LORD hears them; he delivers them from all their troubles. The LORD is close to the brokenhearted and saves those who are crushed in spirit. The righteous person may have many troubles, but the LORD delivers him from them all." (Psalm 34:17-19 NIV)

For those around us who have been blinded by many things

of this world, we need to pray for their deliverance and ask God to reveal things to us so we can learn, understand, and change our perspective on life. We must also take a deep look into our own lives. How many times have we seen others' sins, weaknesses, or lack of understanding, yet overlooked our own?

We need to ask God to reveal to us any imperfections of our own character, our thoughts, words, or actions which are not in line with His Word. Only then will we be able to see things with great clarity and change things that we need to change to be most pleasing in God's eyes.

I am so grateful for my parents determination in keeping us grounded in our faith. I truly don't know what I would have done, or where I would be today, if it was not for my faith and the presence of God in my life. With my parents love and guidance to enlighten and strengthen my faith in God, I was driven to seek a deeper understanding of God's plans and purposes for my life.

My heart, my eyes and ears opened wide, allowing God to work within me and to educate and strengthen me along my spiritual journey. As the days, weeks, months and years passed, I gained such life changing revelations and a deeper understanding and appreciation for what God, Jesus Christ and the Holy Spirit have done and continue to do, in my life and in the lives of all the faithful children of God.

Being passionate about my desire to share of God's love and miraculous works, led me to the writing of this book. Publishing this book enables me to share my life experiences, many blessings, testimonies and revelations.

With patience and faith in God, His Word and promises for all faithful believers, we can all experience and obtain such an amazing love, tremendous peace and optimum courage to face the world.

Since childhood, I believe I had a deep rooted desire to believe there is good in everyone. I believe God was already working within me.

I would like to share with you a few examples of why I believe I was destined (or born) to believe and steered away from anyone or anything that tried to corrupt or detour my thoughts, beliefs or actions, which in turn could hinder my destiny.

I often wondered if my actions were pleasing to God and if I reflected the love of Christ throughout my life. As I looked back and reflected on events in my life and on journal entries I had written, I can see how the Holy Spirit was already guiding my thoughts, words and interactions with others.

For example, I remember having low self-esteem when I was young. Many kids at school would tease me because they said I was ugly, because I was of heavier build, because I wore glasses and because I never had fancy or designer fashions in those days.

Even though I felt ashamed and hurt by the ongoing comments, I didn't get bitter enough to voice hurtful comments back. Believe it or not, I was afraid to hurt their feelings. I learned to ignore the negative remarks and embraced the fact that my family and God loved me just the way I was.

There were still times when discrediting comments would creep back into my thoughts, which evoked feelings of not being pretty enough. This in turn, left me feeling self-conscious and sometimes depressed. During these times I tried to turn my focus onto positive attributes about myself so I wouldn't be inclined to dwell on the negative words and actions of others.

Through self-reflection, I learned more about my intrinsic character and how God designed us all with unique traits, talents, skills and abilities. Taking this time to meditate on my beliefs, values and life purpose, led to a heightened appreciation of who I am, where I have been, and in God's for my future.

Knowing how hurtful words and actions can impact someone's life like it had mine, it hurt me to see others being mistreated in any way. Therefore, when I saw someone being bullied, teased or harassed, my heart was led to step in on their behalf; defending and comforting them the best way I knew how. I hadn't realized at such a young age that I was already developing Christ-like characteristics within me in by showing love, care and compassion for others.

I believe this insightful and genuine passion to be of service to others, was something God planned and purposed for my life long before my birth. My desire to be more like Christ in nature and character, and my passion for blessing others' lives in whatever way I can, I feel is what I was born to believe in and spiritually driven to fulfil in my lifetime.

I also believe God's purpose for my life is to help enlighten and encourage others into a relationship with Him and to share of Christ's love in hopes of drawing others to Him so they too can experience such an amazing love and inner peace.

In Jesus' Holy Name, I pray that the eyes, ears and heart of the lost are open and receptive to the leading of the Holy Spirit. I pray they turn from darkness (the destructive power of satan), into the light (a life entrusted to the power of God), so they may be led into a purpose driven life destined by God. Amen!

John 8:12 (NIV) tells us, *"When Jesus spoke again to the people, he said, "I am the light of the world. Whoever follows me will never walk in darkness, but will have the light of life."*

The pure and bright radiating light of Jesus Christ will guide us as we continue our spiritual walk throughout life's journey.

I would like to share two journal entries with you in which Christ's illuminating light was revealed deep within my heart.

On Monday, September 7, 2010, I began to pray and read God's Word. I then sat back and reflected on God's message and thanked Him for His wonderful words of wisdom and truth. When I finished my devotion, I glanced over at a candle that was lit. It was awesome to see how clear the wax was. I could see clear to the bottom of the holder. For me, it was symbolic of Christ's love for us. His love clearly radiates from heaven to the base of our heart, spirit and soul. There showed no blemish or cloudiness, just bright illuminating light! It was amazing to see how God chose this way to express His deep love for me. I then continued on reading God's Word and gave thanks and praise to Our Lord, Jesus Christ – THE LIGHT OF THE WORLD.

Later as I went to bed, I thought about how I never imagined that I could feel such a deep love that brings tears to my eyes, joy to my heart and uplifts me beyond words could ever describe. His amazing love provides me with such a great feeling of self-worth and sense of purpose in my life. The love was so powerful and strong, I just wanted to get up and sing, dance and share of this fabulous joy and love with others. A love so divine, growing stronger and deeper day by day. HOW GREAT IS HIS LOVE!!!

On Tuesday, September 8, 2010, as I was listening to a Michael W. Smith CD, I came across one song in particular called "The Throne" that really touched my heart. In the lyrics, it mentions a throne of crystal light which reminded me of the bright light and clear wax I had seen in the candle the day before. For me, this was not a coincidence. I believe it was a confirming message from God. Believing God reveals many things to us in a variety of ways, I believe this song was perfectly timed for me to receive His message. I believe God was confirming how we are to have faith in Christ (light of the world), who sits upon Heaven's throne.

Sometimes people continue on in a life of destruction not knowing how to make things right with God, people we have hurt, or our own reconstruction. Through prayer for wisdom and understanding of God's Word and His Will for our life, we can obtain direction through the Holy Spirit which resides in each of us.

When we have a question about a certain topic or decision in our lives, we should seek what the Bible has to say about it. God's written word can provide us with a different perspective on what He is directing for our life. I personally experienced answers from God through meditating on scriptures.

We need to stay focused with utmost patience and a trusting

heart as God directs our steps and brings us to the very place we need to be in our life.

Sometimes God's leading can come through the Holy Spirit, through our conscience and through communications with other people. I found answers and confirmation from God through lyrics in a song, messages shared during church and spiritual services, reading of Christian and other faith-based books, conversations with family and friends and through messages relayed during a movie I was watching.

If we are persistent in prayer, listen attentively and trust God to provide answers to our questions and life circumstances, we will receive our answers at the exact time, and in the exact way, God sets forth for us to receive it.

Some people are often blind to the many blessings around them. We are in a great country, yet how many stop and thank God for the blessing of our freedom? Too many people take for granted the air we breathe, the beauty of nature, the sky and even the ground we walk on. How many times do we ourselves get caught up in the unpleasant things that are happening in our life that we forget to refocus our thoughts and give thanks for all the special blessings that we do have?

At times some people even become "spiritually" blind. They don't understand God's ways; in how we are to live our life in accordance with His commandments.

Living in a world where man's wisdom and abilities are praised and glorified, many people cannot perceive the most basic truths; that all things are made possible through the power and will of God, not through any power of our own abilities.

Many are blinded by their own pleasures, desires for power, or by the pursuit of money and material gains that they lose sight of an even greater reward – salvation and eternal life. Our soul is worth more than this world could ever offer us. Our soul is going to continue to live on forever throughout eternity. Therefore, we cannot afford to lose it into everlasting punishment by making desires of this world our priority in life.

Jesus says in Matthew 16:26 (NLT), *"And what do you benefit if you gain the whole world but lose your own soul? Is anything worth more than your soul?"*

Instead of being self-absorbed in our own ideas and shadowed plans for our life, we need to put our life, our needs and our heart in God's hands, so He can carry out His will in us. We need to keep our focus on what God wants for us so we are able to achieve His plans and purpose for our life. We also need to have complete faith, trust and belief that God does have a set plan and a set future for our life, as well as, a set time in which all of these plans will manifest in our life. God will faithfully see everything through until completion.

As a Christian, I have developed a heart for God, wanting to live to please Him for the rest of my life. By holding fast to His commandments and His Word, I will not allow the ways of the world to corrupt my mind, my words, or my actions. I have made a conscious choice to not allow satan and his destructive ways to blind me, keep me in bondage, or hinder me in any way from receiving God's blessing in my life.

Scripture tells us in James 4:7 (NIV), *"Submit yourselves, then, to God. Resist the devil, and he will flee from you."*

I believe that our unwavering faithfulness to God holds the right key for our future home in His Kingdom. I also believe that those who faithfully continue to walk in the ways of our God will be blessed in reaching their ultimate goals and destination.

To walk in the ways of God, means we have made a heartfelt choice to enter into a relationship with God through faith in Christ, and we are attentive and consistent in seeking to please Him by living our life in accordance with His commandments.

$\mathcal{C}$HAPTER 3

GOD'S TALKING, WHO'S LISTENING?

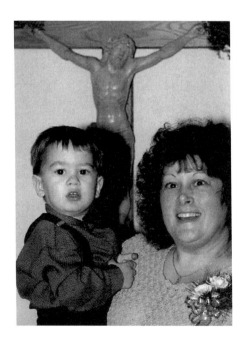

   In hopes of bringing awareness of God's constant presence in our lives even when we least expect Him, I wrote a poem entitled, "God's talking, who's listening?"

God's Talking, Who's Listening?

There are miracles happening
Each day you can see,
Like a medical breakthrough
Or the healthy birth of a baby.

You can be truly enlightened
Through the power of prayer,
And with patience and trust
God will provide your answer.

For each and every one of us,
He has been there all along,
If you listen very carefully,
He could answer through a song.

Through many books or dreams,
People's words or actions,
God continues to speak,
But who really stops and listens?

~

Many people get so bogged down with their daily schedules or personal responsibilities that they have not set time aside to sit back, relax and talk with God. Many of us take time to pray, but have not set time aside to give thanks, reflect, meditate, or clear our heart and mind in preparation for God's response.

God desires for us to communicate with Him. Therefore, it is important for us to be ready at all times for Him to communicate with us. When we still our mind from everything else around us and trust God to provide direction and answers to our prayers, we see how God uses a variety of ways and means to relay His message to us.

God's voice has great power to bring us out of any mental,

physical, financial or spiritual struggles or situations that we may be in. By putting our faith and trust in God, our situations and paths in life can be straightened or turned around, so we can walk with clarity and assurance into what God has planned for our lives.

God provides great words of wisdom and guidance which are communicated to us through His written word. When we read and meditate on His Word, God will reveal meaningful things to us.

Throughout my spiritual journey, I found that journaling my testimonies of what God has revealed to me and how He helped me to overcome obstacles in my life, serves as a great resource for me to reflect back on.

Journaling provides a glimpse into my heart, my passions and my life journey, which I hope will enlighten and inspire future generations into establishing a personal relationship with God.

I would like to share a journal entry with you dated February 27, 2011. I had suffered bouts of anxiety throughout my childhood years into my adult life. One of the root causes for the flare-ups of anxiety was when I was sick. When I had migraine headaches or was sick with asthma symptoms for example, it would stir up thoughts about death and dying.

Ever since grade school years, I remember thinking about what happens to us when we die, who would die first in my family, and how I would be all alone if I died first. I knew that nobody would be going with me and that I would be leaving everybody I loved behind. I spent many years in fear of the unknown and often cried myself to sleep. I did not understand at the time that God is forever present in the lives of His faithful children and at no time would I ever be all alone.

I remember telling my mother about being afraid to die and she said, "Why would you be afraid of that now, you are young and healthy, most people don't die until their old age, you have many years ahead of you". That calmed my anxiety for the most part, but as the years went on, the anxiety seemed to heighten. It was so hard for me to figure out why these feelings were so strong and dominated my thinking.

In speaking with my friend Pam, she and I prayed to God for enlightenment as to the root causes of these fears and anxieties. About a week after diligently praying and speaking with God, much was revealed to me today (February 27, 2011). As I was in church, my pastor was preaching about heavenly rewards. I hadn't realized until today that a great source of my anxiety stemmed from what happens to our soul when we die.

I strive to be the best person I can be by reflecting Christ-like characteristics through my thoughts, words and actions. Plus, the Bible tells us we receive salvation through Christ as Romans 10:9-10 (NIV) tells us, *"If you declare with your mouth, 'Jesus is Lord,' and believe in your heart that God raised him from the dead, you will be saved. For it is with your heart that you believe and are justified, and it is with your mouth that you profess your faith and are saved."* Yet, why was I still afraid of death?

Fear of the unknown about what happens to us after death haunted me for many years. I had unsettling thoughts about whether our soul or spirit, just floated among others in the kingdom, which left me with much confusion as to how I would really be united with others who passed on before me.

As the pastor continued speaking, she quoted Scriptures that provided me with great peace and trust to successfully deal with the anxieties and fears I had experienced for so many years regarding the unknown after death.

2 Corinthians 5:1 (NLT) tells us, *"For we know that when this earthly tent we live in is taken down (that is, when we die and leave this earthly body), we will have a house in heaven, an eternal body made for us by God himself and not by human hands."*

"For we will put on heavenly bodies; we will not be spirits without bodies." 2 Corinthians 5:3 (NLT)

I give great thanks and praise to Jesus Christ for our salvation into the kingdom of heaven and I will share my testimonies with others in love and thanks for how I have been transformed by the renewing of my mind, heart and spirit.

In talking with my cousin Debbie later that same day, I was sharing the message the pastor was speaking about at church regarding heaven. I explained to her how I hadn't realized that the uncertainties of eternal life had impacted my thinking - generating feelings of fear and anxiety. I also shared that I have been praying to find out the original source of my fears of dying.

Debbie opened my eyes to another factor that I believe was another root cause of my fears and anxiety regarding death. The fear of God that I grew to know since childhood was not a fear that inspired or encouraged me to draw nearer to Him. For me, it was the opposite. I seemed to have pulled back.

I remember being taught since childhood years that if we used a curse word, lied, neglected to pray or go to church, or if didn't go to confession, we were told it was a sin and we would go to hell. I recall being reminded in great depth that we would inevitably pay for our sins in the fires of hell.

I also remember if anyone said a bad word, one of the first things another playmate would say is, "you're going to go to hell because you said a bad word". Memories of other children telling us that we would go to hell or to purgatory exasperated what I had already believed to be true. Sometimes it is difficult to shake some childhood memories or words that had such a profound effect on our thinking and on our beliefs.

I believe I hadn't yet developed an understanding that if we do love God as He loves us, we should desire to do things to please Him and show great respect for who He is, for what He has done and continues to do in our lives. I believe this would have helped me to understand that we need to do the right things in the eyes of God because of our love and respect for Him, not because of an overwhelming fear of going to hell.

I believe I did not have a true fear of God and feared that I may not be worthy of eternal life in heaven. Let me explain…

Throughout the years I remember thinking how I was destined for hell because I hadn't attended church for quite some time and I no longer went to confession since my late teenage years. I also remember feeling that God would definitely punish us for our sins, or if we died before our sins had been forgiven, we would go to "purgatory".

Can you imagine as a child, being told purgatory was a place, or state of being, where we would go temporarily to cleanse us of our sins and prepare us for heaven. In believing this to be true, great fear and confusion existed; thinking we would be kept in limbo or we would be floating around somewhere, not good enough to go to heaven yet not bad enough to go to hell.

I experienced how fear can paralyze us to do nothing instead of finding ways to correct our mistakes and to do what is right and pleasing in God's eyes. Because of feeling unworthy to go to heaven and worrying about the uncertainties of purgatory, I had no desire at that time to know God better. As a result, there was many times I even felt paralyzed as to where to turn for help. I believe the feeling of not being worthy of eternal life with God is what has been deep rooted into my brain from a very young age, causing a great part of anxiety in my life.

I was grateful for Debbie bringing this to my attention. I do believe teachers, school counsellors and others who wanted to guide our steps down the right path in life taught us the best they knew how from their own upbringing and personal experiences in regards to faith and spirituality, but I believe sometimes the focus was more on religious customs, beliefs and practices, instead of focusing on God's character, His Word, His love, and on the importance of building a faithful relationship with Him, bringing forth a true fear of God.

I know it was not a coincidence that Debbie visited this afternoon. I believe God had spoken through her as well as the pastor today in helping me to understand the root causes of my fear of dying which generated great anxiety throughout the years. I thank God with all my heart for this new revelation today! I am so blessed to have been led by the Holy Spirit into developing a greater love and understanding of God and His Word.

I have not found any reference in Scriptures as to a place called purgatory. In my opinion, such teaching as this relays a message that Christ's suffering and death on the cross was not satisfactory enough. We read otherwise in various scriptures in the Bible.

Scriptures tell us that because of Christ's sacrifice, we are already cleansed, forgiven, redeemed, restored, purified, and declared righteous. Therefore, why would anyone have to go to purgatory after death for cleansing or purification?

In reading the Bible, God tells us how Christ died to redeem us from ALL ours sins, not just some of our sins.

"But he was pierced for our rebellion, crushed for our sins. He was beaten so we could be whole. He was whipped so we could be healed. All of us, like sheep, have strayed away. We have left God's paths to follow our own. Yet the Lord laid on him the sins of us all." Isaiah 53:5-7 (NLT)

God tells us in Scripture that if we are truly sorry for our sins, repent of them, turn away from our sinful ways to follow Him, our sins will be forgiven.

"Now repent of your sins and turn to God, so that your sins may be wiped away." Acts 3:19 (NLT)

Some religions teach that salvation is achieved through our good works here on earth. Holding to this view, we would never know for sure if we will receive salvation because there is no way to know for sure if the good works we do will be sufficient enough.

The Bible tells us with certainty that we cannot earn our salvation through good deeds that we do, because Jesus' death on the cross paid for all our sin so that we may receive salvation and life everlasting with Him. We find confirmation to this truth in the following scriptures:

Eph. 2:8-9 (NIV) – *"For it is by grace you have been saved, through faith—and this is not from yourselves, it is the gift of God— not by works, so that no one can boast."*

Roman 5:1-2 (NLT) -*"Therefore, since we have been made right in God's sight by faith, we have peace with God because of what Jesus Christ our Lord has done for us. Because of our faith, Christ has brought us into this place of undeserved privilege where we now stand, and we confidently and joyfully look forward to sharing God's glory."*

By continuing to hold firm to God's Word, it has allowed me to obtain such great peace and freedom, and has inspired me to shine God's love in all I do and say to help bring others into a special relationship with God that will truly bless their lives in more ways than they can even imagine.

During a visit with another dear friend, I was asked if my fear of unworthiness for eternal life in heaven, could have stemmed from thinking that I did something wrong in God's eyes, by leaving my former church (which I attended since childhood) to now attend a Non-Denominational Christian Church.

As I reflected on what my friend asked, I came to realize that the uncertainty as to whether leaving my former church would be acceptable in my family's eyes and in the eyes God, left me with feelings of confusion and guilt. On one hand, I felt like I was deserting my family by moving on in my spiritual journey without them, and on the other hand, I wasn't sure if attending this new church was where God was leading me to, or if it stemmed from my own desires to explore something new.

Again I needed to trust that God would lead my heart where He needed me to be; enabling me to strengthen my faith along my spiritual journey with Him.

Although the initial transition to another Church had me questioning whether this is where God wants me to be, I soon believed that this is exactly where God was leading me. I soon felt great peace, inspiration, enlightenment, love, happiness, comfort, and a great sense of belonging. I believe the Holy Spirit was confirming God's answer that I am where I need to be at this point in my life.

God revealed a very important message to me in regards to whether leaving my former church would be acceptable in my family's eyes. I received His message quite clearly as I read Mother Teresa's "Anyway" poem. Mother Teresa's message expressed in her poem was in reference to doing good even though our efforts seem to look bleak. The last two lines of her poem especially touched my heart and reminded me of one great truth in life, "You see, in the final analysis, it is between you and God; It was never between you and them anyway."

What great words of wisdom expressed by Mother Teresa. She is absolutely right. What we do in life is between us and God. We need to take our focus off of what others may think of us and our choices and concentrate on what God has to say; beings it is ultimately between Him and us anyways.

As the weeks and months went by, I gained greater understanding and insight into God's Word and His desires for our life as Christians. I experienced amazing love and renewed energy to seek a deeper and more meaningful relationship with God.

Through enhanced wisdom and understanding obtained along my spiritual journey, I was able to let go of fears, uncertainties and guilt that once held me back.

I continue to trust God in leading my heart to His destined path for my spiritual growth and in fulfilling his plans and purposes in my life. I believe God places each and every one of us right where He needs us to be to grow along our journey with Him.

Another deep rooted fear of mine, especially in regards to death, was the fear of being alone. I could not figure out where these fears of being alone originated because I was never ever left alone when I was young, nor was I ever lost in a mall or anything of that sort. The only thing I knew of was the thoughts of being alone in death. I again prayed to God for clarification and understanding, trusting that He would answer my prayers as I continue to diligently seek Him for guidance and listen wholeheartedly for His answer.

I believe that one of the reasons why I strongly feared that I would be alone when I die was because of feelings I experienced during grade school years. Stressed upon us at such an impressionable age was how we are to behave, or we would have to suffer the consequences of going to hell. If I felt that I was unworthy to go to heaven at that time, I must have believed consciously or sub-consciously, that I was most likely going to hell and would not have the presence of God, Jesus Christ or any loved ones with me. What a great burden for anyone to feel in their lifetime no matter what age.

While attending church service one Sunday in March of 2011, the pastor played a short video clip on Satan and how he gets people to believe his lies, trying to get them to pull away from their faith and from their trust in God. In the video clip Satan was training one of his evil followers on how to trap people and make them feel like there is no hope or any way out of their past or present circumstances.

Satan expressed to his followers, how he likes to prey on the minds of people who are already burdened, especially those who are extremely weak and vulnerable. He went on to explain how he repeats over and over again in their minds that they are useless, they will never get out of the situation they are in, that life isn't worth living, or even that they are alone in this world because there is no one to help them. Satan stated that by attacking people when they are weak, he can get them to believe his lies and pull them away from trusting and believing in God.

I believe Satan was trying all along to get me to feel like I was all alone and that I was helpless and weak. He was determined to stir up feelings of depression or anxiety by getting me to focus on all his lies. By occupying my mind with so many other things, I believe Satan hoped to distract me from focusing on my trust and faith in God.

What really hit me today is that I believe Satan repetitively put these lies into my head throughout the years and they got deep rooted in the back of my mind and would resurface especially when I was ill or burdened by other traumatic events that occurred in my life.

When we read the bible, we come to understand how Satan always had, and continues to have, an insatiable desire for supremacy. He desires the power and glory which belongs to God alone.

In reading God's Word, I came to understand how Satan uses the fear of death to keep us in bondage. Hebrew 2:14-15 (NLT) tells us, *"Because God's children are human beings—made of flesh and blood—the Son also became flesh and blood. For only as a human being could he die, and only by dying could he break the power of the devil, who had the power of death. Only in this way could he set free all who have lived their lives as slaves to the fear of dying."*

As I reflected on this scripture, I came to believe that Satan was the root cause of my fear of dying. I believe the thoughts of being unworthy of eternal life with God, was deep rooted into my brain by Satan. Knowing my passion to deepen my relationship and faith in, I believe Satan used the fear of dying ever since I was young, to provoke great anxiety and keep me in bondage.

Therefore, when Satan tries to corrupt our mind with the fear of dying, fear of being alone, fear of the unknown, we must cancel these thoughts right away and remind Satan of God's Word and promises for our lives.

What really helped and continues to help me overcome bouts of anxiety and uneasiness in my spirit, is in reciting 2 Timothy 1:7 (NLT) - *"For God has not given us a spirit of fear and timidity, but of power, love, and self-discipline."* By doing so, I continue to remind Satan that he has no power or control over me anymore. At the same time, I give praise and thanks to God for gifting my life with the spirit of power, love and self-discipline.

God will not let us be tempted beyond what we can bear as expressed in 1 Corinthians 10:13 (NIV) - *"No temptation has overtaken you except what is common to mankind. And God is faithful; he will not let you be tempted beyond what you can bear. But when you are tempted, he will also provide a way out so that you can endure it."*

What great peace and freedom we can obtain by educating ourselves on God's Word and holding firm in faith and obedience to God. We can then gain greater insight and assurance of God's presence and endless love forever in our lives.

I trust God will be with me throughout my life tests and that He will help me to grow stronger and deeper in trusting faith of my destiny and eternal life with Him.

CHAPTER 4

CONFIRMING WORDS OF GOD

In order for us to fully understand God's communication with us, we must diligently read, study, and meditate on His Word. As we read in the Bible, we see that Jesus prayed often and was in constant communication with His Father. As Christians, we are to do the same as Jesus did.. We must have trusting faith in God our Father to answer our prayers as He answered those of Jesus' and many others as expressed in several scriptures of the Bible.

I would like to share a heartwarming experience that I journalized in February of 2009. This was truly an enlightening and comforting experience which helped to strengthen my trust and faith in God's amazing presence in our lives.

I had debated about whether or not to attend an upcoming encounter weekend. A couple of weeks prior to the encounter weekend I felt an overwhelming desire in my spirit to go to the encounter class being held after service. In hearing the message shared during the service that day, I felt strongly that this was the perfect time for me to attend the encounter weekend.

During the encounter weekend, we watched a video clip from "The Passion of the Christ" movie by Mel Gibson. Throughout the weekend, we were encouraged to express our feelings openly as we heart was being led to do. Myself and others at the encounter chose to go up to the Cross at the front of the room and gave thanks and praise to Our Lord Jesus Christ. The song "Nothing but the Blood of Jesus" was beautifully sung as we proceeded back to our seat. I got instant chills. What better way to express the love of Christ and the power in The Blood of Jesus.

I believe it was not a coincidence, but a confirmation from God, that it was the Holy Spirit leading me to attend this encounter weekend. I had been singing that very song over and over in my head for a quite few days prior to that weekend. I often woke up singing this song and sometimes began singing in part way through my day. Although I love this song, I didn't know why I just automatically starting singing this song for many days in a row instead of singing other spiritual songs that I often listen to on CD or the radio. I believe God was preparing my spiritual eyes, ears heart and mind to be open and receptive to the depth of Christ's love. What Christ endured on our behalf. There is no greater love!

I know this is a difficult movie to watch in regards to the suffering of Christ on our behalf, but I remember thinking that if Christ endured all this agony on my behalf, I can at least try to watch it to bring about a deeper understanding and appreciation for all He has done and continues to do for us. What an amazing love He has shown us and continues to show us throughout our life journey.

I feel that no matter what I face in my lifetime, it will never compare to what Christ had to endure. God Our Father was with Jesus throughout His life journey and I believe and trust in God's promise to be with us also. I thank you Father God, for Your confirming words, endless love and ongoing faith strengthening revelations!!!

Many people may not experience the fullness of life because of fears, pain or hindrances operating in their lives. Attending an encounter weekend can help bring about a renewed and heightened understanding, healing and peace in our lives. I found it to be a truly rewarding experience.

Christ's passion for healing the sick and bringing salvation to all is a true indication of His ultimate love for all mankind. What a great role model for all of us to learn great patience, compassion, unselfishness and unconditional love. By modelling the nature and character of Christ, we are truly relaying to others how we desire to love God wholeheartedly.

I would like to share another testimony of God's confirming words with you that I journalized on September 4, 2009. After reading God's Word, I closed my eyes to focus on God, waiting for Him to speak to me. The words, "Humble yourself with a contrite heart" came into my spirit as well as the words "love lifts us up where we belong". I then focused on why God was telling me these words at this particular time. I picked up my Bible to see what God needed to reveal to me today. I believe God wanted me to read in Isaiah 57.

"…I restore the crushed spirit of the humble and revive the courage of those with repentant hearts." Isaiah 57:15 (NLT)

By knowing the forgiveness of sins we received through the crucifixion of Jesus Christ and by acknowledging and confessing our sins now before God, we can then leave all the guilt, burdens or heart ache we felt at the foot of the cross. God promises us, as seen in the scripture above, that He will restore our crushed spirit and revive courage within us if we do sincerely repent of our sins. We can then begin to move on in life with a peaceful heart and open mind to receive all that God has planned for our lives.

I do believe God wanted me to focus on this today in confirmation of His forgiveness of my sins because of my repentance, which in turn allows me to let go of my past. By holding on to past issues, we are kept in bondage which ends up blocking God's blessings from manifesting in our lives. I also believe God was revealing to me that by humbling myself before Him, He will provide me with a renewed heart, mind and spirit to fulfil all that He has in store for my life.

I believe the song "Love Lifts Us Up Where We Belong", written by Joe Cocker and sung by him and Jennifer Warnes, came to me in confirmation of God's previous words in humbling myself before Him. Love does lift us up to great new heights. When we humble ourselves before God, His unfailing love keeps us above this world of sin and wickedness and provides a clear heart, mind and spirit for all believers. What a powerful message I received today through the working of the Holy Spirit in my life.

I do believe that our roads (our life journey) may seem very long and trying at times, and the mountains (or struggles, pathways and challenges) may be blocking our way to move ahead in life, but through faith, we can continue to climb (or grow) more and more every day.

God is faithful to guide us and help us to reach our goals and in achieving all His plans and purposes that He has destined for our lives. What a powerful and combined message revealed to me today. Thank you God for your continuing confirmation and wonderful words!

$\mathcal{C}$HAPTER 5

TRUST IN JESUS,
OUR SAVIOUR AND HEALER

I would like to share a testimony of Thanks to Our Lord, Jesus Christ for all He has done, all He continues to do, and for everything He represents.

Through a special friend of mine, I was introduced to a whole new world of truth and divine love. First through Our Lord, Jesus Christ, and then witnessed in other believers, leaders and Pastors alike.

I was baptized (as an adult) on March 19, 2006. My need for spiritual growth and enhanced wisdom and understanding of God's Word and plans and purposes for my life, had greatly intensified.

I heard of a Healing Class being offered in May of 2009 at a local church for which my heart felt driven to attend. I found the profound teaching from the leader, the content of material used in the class, and the promises of our Lord Jesus Christ, to be so powerful and inspirational. There was great focus on mental, physical and spiritual well-being.

During the healing classes, I was enlightened to how we as

Christian, have the power to take authority over our illnesses and over our circumstances; in The Name of Jesus. This is the first time in my life that I learned of such a great power we can possess as true believers and children of God.

I was experiencing extreme pain in my right knee due to a tear in the cartilage, and surgery to repair it was booked for November of 2009. After learning a great deal about the power we obtain through our words and actions as true believers in Jesus Christ, I cancelled the surgery. I put my trust in God's healing power. Through the power of prayer in Jesus' Holy Name, I was confident I would receive complete healing.

By October of 2009, I was pain free from my knee injury and to this day, I have not and do not, experience any pain whatsoever due to that injury. Whether big or small, God's miraculous healing forever lives on!

I believe that once I accepted Jesus Christ as my Lord and Saviour and was baptized as an adult, greater things began to happen in my life.

When I learned to trust in Christ in all areas of my life, beginning with His forgiveness of my sins; my values, behaviours and thinking were cleansed from all that was not in line with God's Word. I was guided by the Holy Spirit into a great renewing of my mind, heart and spirit.

Through the wisdom and understanding I received from the Holy Spirit working within me, many times I was left in awe as to what I experienced, what I heard, and from what was revealed to me through my dreams and visions.

When I entrusted everything in my life to Christ, I felt tremendous burdens lifted from my shoulders. I finally found great inner peace, strength and courage to face life and all its challenges because I knew I was not alone to face whatever came my way.

When we study God's Word, we see so often how Christ

saved and healed all who were of great faith. By submitting our life to Jesus Christ, He will guide us into a renewed life which is in accordance with God's Will.

When we come to learn what is expected of us in our life journey, we must trust and rely on Christ's strength and power to do these things through the working of the Holy Spirit within us. I am so grateful for this understanding and for this new beginning in life; allowing me to follow on the right path for achieving everlasting happiness and eternal rewards through a great leader, healer and Saviour, Jesus Christ!

Christ tells us in John 14:6 (NIV), *"I am the way and the truth and the life. No one comes to the Father except through me."*

We also read in the bible how God performed many miracles when the Apostles used the name of Jesus in faith, believing wholeheartedly in the power of His name.

Mark 16:17-18 (NLT), *"These miraculous signs will accompany those who believe: They will cast out demons in my name, and they will speak in new languages. They will be able to handle snakes with safety, and if they drink anything poisonous, it won't hurt them. They will be able to place their hands on the sick, and they will be healed."*

We are reminded in this scripture that we need to trust in Christ as the way, truth and life and that we cannot go to the Father except through Him. This has helped me to understand and associate the power we can have in prayer by speaking the Name of Jesus Christ over our petitions.

By trusting in Jesus' Name and in His Blood to bring about miraculous healing, deliverance, and answers to our prayers, we can patiently wait and trust that He will hear and respond to our needs.

There are no words to express my true appreciation. Therefore, I will let my words and actions speak for me. I truly desire to be more Christ-like; more patient, unselfish, more compassionate, understanding, non-judgmental, and all that Jesus Christ Himself represents.

I will continue to share of my time, talents, words of encouragement, God's Word and my testimonies with others, to help draw them into a special relationship with God so they too can know of such a powerful and unfailing love.

I wrote a poem on May 9, 2010 to express my confidence and trust in God, Jesus Christ and the Holy Spirit. My heart was so full of love and appreciation for all they have done and continue to do.

A Faithful Trust

With utmost confidence I pray
For the Holy Spirit to light my way,
So my thoughts, my words and my actions
Will be a blessing for other's each day.

As my faith continues to grow stronger,
The fears I felt are no longer.
For understanding to complete my true life's purpose,
It's divine wisdom from God that I hunger.

With secured faith and love in my heart
From God's continuing embrace I will never part.
To be the best person that I could be,
Was truly my soul mission from the very start.

When life gets too tough and challenging,
I can always rely on Jesus for everything.
For whatever burden's too heavy to carry,
It's our prayers for help He is waiting.

~

I give utmost thanks to God, and pray for all leaders, Priests, Ministers, Pastors, and all women and men of God who continue to educate us on God's Word; on the life, death, and teachings of Jesus Christ; and on the importance of the Holy Spirit in our lives.

After experiencing such tremendous strength and courage to overcome many challenges and a few traumatic life experiences, I gained an unshakeable trust, immense love and appreciation for all God has done and continues to do for me, my family, friends, and all His beloved children. My heart is comforted in knowing I am never alone. God is always with me throughout my life journey.

Hebrews 12:1-6 (NLT) tells us, *"… since we are surrounded by such a huge crowd of witnesses to the life of faith, let us strip off every weight that slows us down, especially the sin that so easily trips us up. And let us run with endurance the race God has set before us. We do this by keeping our eyes on Jesus, the champion who initiates and perfects our faith."*

> *MAY GOD SHINE HIS HEAVENLY BLESSINGS*
> *UPON EACH AND EVERY ONE OF US*
> *AS WE CONTINUE OUR LIFE JOURNEY*
> *WITH UNWAVERING PASSION AND PURPOSE*
> *TO SEEK AND ACHIEVE*
> *ALL HE DESTINED FOR YOU AND ME.*
> *IN JESUS' NAME I PRAY. AMEN!*

$\mathcal{C}$HAPTER 6

REFLECTING THE LOVE OF JESUS

Early on in life, I remember my mother telling us how important it is to be respectful and kind to everyone. She explained how hurtful and disrespectful it is to laugh at, or make fun of others. Mom continued to explain how we would want others to love us for who we are. She posed the following question to us as children, "How would you feel if others ignored you or were unkind to you because you were different in any way.?"

Mom also shared a scripture that she wanted us to remember throughout our life time. Luke 6:31 (NIV), *"Do to others as you would have them do to you."* Believing in God's commands for our life, she wanted to express how we are to love others in accordance with God's Word and His will for our life. These shared words from Mom served as a conscious reminder of how we are to share the love of Christ by respecting people of all cultures, races, varying statuses, etc.

My grandmother (known to us as Meme), taught us to be non-judgmental of others. I remember sharing some school day stories with her. As I explained how hurtful some kids were being, or how rude they would speak to me and others, she would always turn the negative situations into positive ones. Meme explained how I was not to be rude or disrespectful in return; quoting once again how the Bible tells us to treat others how we would like to be treated and how we are to love others.

John 15:12 (NIV) – *"My command is this: Love each other as I have loved you."*

Ephesians 4:32 (NIV) – *"Be kind and compassionate to one another, forgiving each other, just as in Christ God forgave you."*

1 John 4:20 (NLT) - *If someone says, "I love God," but hates a fellow believer, that person is a liar; for if we don't love people we can see, how can we love God, whom we cannot see?"*

Meme further explained that there could be difficult or abusive situations going on in someone's life that is causing them to react the way they are. She also said that maybe others are lashing out at us, but maybe what they're really looking for is love and kindness and don't know how to express this appropriately to us. What great words of enlightenment!

I always knew my grandmother to be very loving; always expressing and sharing her trusting faith in God. What great examples she shared with us throughout the years so we too could learn Christ-like characteristics early on in our lives. I will always remember those special moments with Meme.

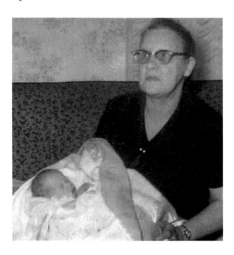

Me with Grandma, (Meme D.)

In 2004, I wrote the following heartfelt poem in loving memory of my grandmother, who was also my Godmother at my baptism as a baby. Meme truly lived up to her role as my godmother. Her commitment to being a good role model by leading her life in unity with the Catholic faith, as well as, her continued support in helping me to grow and strive for spiritual maturity, was truly admirable.

Touch Of An Angel

I remember the days,
Those special times at Meme's.
She touched so many lives
With her experience and ways.

Her many prayers and offerings
And various talents and blessings,
Was like that of an Angel
Who truly earned their wings.

With that touch of an angel,
She helped when I fell.
Without a word of a doubt,
For years, her life I will tell.

With the kindest voice I ever heard,
I did listen to each word,
And kept them dear in my heart,
For I was comforted and assured.

With sincere trust she did say,
On very many a day,
"There's nothing for you to fear,
For God will show you the way."

Throughout my life, I remember sharing her kind words of wisdom with many others. If someone was being ridiculed, bullied, or in need of a friend, I was there to assist and befriend them in the best way I knew how. From that point on, I always wanted to be a compassionate, caring, and loving person like my grandmother because I knew this would please God and it made me feel great to be able to help someone in need.

The following two scriptures clearly explain how we are to treat others in likeness of Christ.

Philippians 2:3-5 (NIV) tells us, *"Do nothing out of selfish ambition or vain conceit. Rather, in humility value others above yourselves, not looking to your own interests but each of you to the interests of the others. In your relationships with one another, have the same mindset as Christ Jesus…"*

We also read in Matthew 25:37-40 (NIV), *"Then the righteous will answer him, 'Lord, when did we see you hungry and feed you, or thirsty and give you something to drink? When did we see you a stranger and invite you in, or needing clothes and clothe you? When did we see you sick or in prison and go to visit you?' The King will reply, 'Truly I tell you, whatever you did for one of the least of these brothers and sisters of mine, you did for me.' "*

As God's Word tells us, we are to remove selfishness, anger, pride, and laziness from our way of thinking and acting to enable us to have the mindset of Christ; showing great compassion and love for one another.

I believe my grandmother genuinely enacted the likeness of Christ in the way she lived her life in service to God, her family and others in need. Even with fourteen children of her own, she generously shared her love, time and abilities in helping others.

Grandma worked for a little while in a hospital as a "candy striper"; as it was called then. I believe it was similar to a nurse's assistance with housekeeping duties attached.

In hearing how working at the hospital provided her with a sense of purpose and life fulfilment, I then decided that I also wanted to have a job that is rewarding to me as hers was to her.

I had a few jobs in my lifetime beginning at age 16, but I

would inevitably end up right back in healthcare (in long-term care nursing homes). I am presently still employed in a long-term care home. It can be a very challenging job at times, but I remember what my heart's desire is: "to reflect the love and characteristics of Jesus with everyone, especially to those in need."

How rewarding it has been for me to see the residents laugh or smile, or to see their bright eyes looking at me. If I could change a feeling of depression, loneliness or sickness, into a feeling of being loved and respected, how great I felt and how pleased I believe God is as He sees us carrying out His command to love one another.

CHAPTER 7

PASSION TO ACHIEVE GOD'S PURPOSE

I would like to share a journal entry of mine dated December 3, 2009. As I was reading the book "Purpose Driven Life" by Rick Warren, I came upon a message that reminded me of a passion I had in 2007. The message in part, pertained to God giving people a godly passion to champion a cause.

In 2007, my passion for helping others in need had grown stronger. Believing God had placed this upon my heart, I prayed and asked God for greater clarity as to whom I was being led to serve. With trust in the Holy Spirit to provide wisdom and understanding as to where God was leading me, my heart and mind remained open; awaiting God's reply.

A few months had passed bye, but it wasn't long afterwards when I began with an intense and unshakeable focus on what I could do to help improve the quality of life for residents in long-term care homes; something over and above my duties as a Health Care Aide. I hadn't realized it at the time, but I do believe this is where God was leading me.

I had worked in long-term care for over 25 years and my desire to help residents who had no voice, residents with cognitive impairments and residents with no family to speak up for them, remained a priority and something I felt driven to fulfill in my lifetime. I knew that something needed to be done to bring awareness to the public about the needs of these residents.

I am so grateful that God blessed me with a co-worker and dear friend, who also had the same heartfelt desire to speak up for these residents and try to make a difference in their quality of life. We were able to get two more co-workers on board with us.

Although I was a Union Chairperson at the time, this was not an attempt to bring attention to our Local Union or to ourselves. It was a personal desire and goal of ours to bring awareness to all people who could make a difference in the care and needs of residents in long-term care.

We understood that repercussions could possibly come about once we went public, but our passion, our love for the residents and our trust in God's guidance along the way, outweighed the risks and outcomes of what we could possibly face because of our efforts.

My co-workers and I believed that we needed to go to the source of where the primary changes must originate from. We set up a meeting with our Provincial and Federal Members of Parliament and expressed our concerns for improvement in healthcare to meet the needs of the residents and to provide them with the rights, dignity and respect that they truly deserve.

Our message during the meeting seemed to be well received. They listened attentively and were very supportive, compassionate and understanding as to the goal we were striving to achieve. Before leaving the meeting, we were asked to write something up in regards to the needs of the residents that could be brought forward to the public during an information picket, for which they agreed to attend.

I felt in my spirit that I should express our intentions through a poem. They reviewed the poem and suggested that it be handed out during our information picket. It read;

Speaking Through Silence

As they lay there so patiently,
With trusting eyes, your smile they see.
They know not what the day will bring
but feel of your love and endless caring.

Through their eyes and gentle touch,
Or from their body gestures and such,
No health care worker can ignore
The importance of what we're here for.

As an advocate for residents so dear
I pray for God's assistance here,
For our health care system and M.P.P.'s
To stop and listen to us please.

It's time to make a difference now,
For I know God will show them how.
With an open mind and heart they'd see
How great our long-term care can be.

If we look inside residents' life paid dues,
To make a difference we must choose.
Too many times we hear money's not there
But what would it take for more to care?

If not at the cost of rights and dignity,
Why are we struggling? You tell me.
We can only do what we do at best
And pray to God to help with the rest.

As family and caregivers we truly understand,
Their final years like this, they had not planned.
As they speak to us through their silence,
To fulfill their needs is what makes sense.

Although it brought no immediate changes, I am grateful that
I listened to my heart and that my friend and two co-workers

joined me to speak up and venture out to government officials and the media to try and bring about necessary changes for these residents.

I believe our actions truly did reflect the love of Jesus. As we read in the Bible, Jesus did not come to be served, but to serve, and to give his life for the salvation of many. Jesus Christ is the perfect example of a man dedicating His life to serving others. God desires us to model our lives like Christ in how we are to serve others in our lifetime.

I know and trust that God is a miracle working God and that He will not leave His people who cry out to Him for help. I believe He has heard our pleas and they have not gone unnoticed. God continues to do wonderful things through various people and through various means.

During elections that same year, a minimum standard of care for residents in long-term care was placed on the platform of one of the political parties to address a majority of their needs.

Inevitably, the greatest changes will come according to God's will, in God's time. I thank Him for all He has done through the years and for what He is still about to.

I continue to pray for guidance and direction to fulfil whatever plans and purposes God has planned for me at my workplace and in my personal life.

I believe God confirmed that my passion for speaking up for the elderly was a predestined plan for my life. This confirmation came to me as I read Proverbs 31:8-9 (NIV) – *"Speak up for those who cannot speak for themselves, for the rights of all who are destitute. Speak up and judge fairly; defend the rights of the poor and needy."*

Throughout my life, I often questioned myself as to whether people do really see the love of Christ through me. I desire to please Him and glorify Him for all He has done for us. Therefore, I will testify of His love and endless blessings throughout the days and years to come.

CHAPTER 8

RELAXING YOUR HEART AND MIND

I would like to share a journal entry dated Monday, May 24, 2010. The night before I wrote this entry, I began thanking God for the wonderful day I had. With a warm sense of peace and love in my heart, I felt so completely relaxed. I began to think about how many years it has taken for me to be able to clear my mind of all thoughts; enabling my mind, body and spirit to be relaxed, renewed and revitalized, so I could confidently face whatever comes my way.

About 10 years ago, I was feeling so overwhelmed by the marital situation I was in and by the many traumatic events that took place in my life, so I just shut my thinking off and focused on nothing. At those particular moments of mental blankness, I questioned myself as to whether or not I was becoming numb to the world and to everything and everybody around me. I never thought much more about it at the time because in those moments, I did feel at peace.

A couple of years ago I shared my thoughts with a friend. I wondered if letting my mind "go numb" was a good thing or not. I told her that I thought it may be a technique I was supposed to learn long ago.

I do believe it was a sign from God, working through the Holy Spirit. I believe He was trying to take me to a place where I would be able to clear my mind from all the worldly things around me so I could focus on Him. I believe God helped me to achieve this relaxation technique so I would be more receptive in hearing from Him with greater clarity.

When our attention is not focused on our troubles, fears or jobs, we leave ourselves open to obtain a greater understanding of God and His plans and purposes for our life. We need to make time for God. Time to thank Him for all His blessings, time to worship Him, time to pray to Him, and especially time to be patient to wait and listen for Him to speak to us.

I seemed to have achieved a lifelong challenge in being able to come to a new chapter in my life, where I could totally relax my mind, body and spirit. However, it was not by my power, but by God's power and the presence of the Holy Spirit that guided my every step in achieving such great peace. I know I wasn't in this journey alone.

If we make an honest effort to rid ourselves of everything going on around us and find a quiet place to relax and meditate, I believe this would enhance not only our relationship with God, but also with Jesus Christ and the Holy Spirit. In Colossians 2:6-7 and 2 Corinthians 13:14 (NLT), we see read how God desires us to have trust and unwavering faith in Him, Jesus Christ and the Holy Spirit.

As I was writing this journal entry today, I came across inspiring Scriptures that embrace my testimony of the inner peace I was destined to learn and obtain for my life.

"The LORD replied, *'My Presence will go with you, and I will give you rest.'* " Exodus 33:14 (NIV)

John 14:26-27 (NIV) tells us - "...*the Advocate, the Holy Spirit, whom the Father will send in my name, will teach you all things and will remind you of everything I have said to you. Peace I leave with you; my peace I give you. I do not give to you as the world gives. Do not let your hearts be troubled and do not be afraid."*

Who knew at the times I felt my weakest, I was actually my strongest. God kept me by His side and strengthened me mentally, physically and spiritually. Regardless of how tough or impossible a situation or crisis seems to be for us to face on our own, we need to remember that with God all things are possible! This is when we must continue to believe and trust in Him with unshakeable faith.

With the help of the Holy Spirit, I have learned to be more compassionate, understanding and patient. Trusting in the Holy Spirit's presence in my life, I feel an exceptional love, joy and peace, in knowing that God is always with me.

I would like to share two other journal entries confirming the presence of the Holy Spirit working within me; helping me to understand God's messages and direction for my life. By relaxing my heart and mind, and through reflection and meditation, wonderful things were revealed to me.

The first journal entry is dated September 3, 2009. As I began to pray today, I felt such a heartwarming love from God Our Father and tears began to flow as I thanked Him for His many blessings in my life and in my family and friends lives.

I felt a strong presence of the Holy Spirit over me. I experienced great freedom in giving control of my life over to God. As I closed my eyes, I had a vision of God facing me with His hands stretched out to me. I then felt a Big Supernatural Hug, straight from God Himself. At the same time, I heard the words, "Be rest assured with peace in your heart". I felt so filled with peace and love that tears just kept coming. What an awesome and supernatural experience!

I believe God was confirming to me that He has heard and answered my prayers and He has heard my words of thanks and praise for all He's done and continues to do. I believe through this vision, God wanted to reassure me of His continued presence in my life. By doing so, God knew this would strengthen my trust and faith in Him and bring great peace. I believe God was also telling me to be "rest assured" - assured of His love, His protection, His guidance and His blessings. With God forever present and in control, there is nothing for me to fear.

I had often read how God can and does bless our lives far beyond our own imaginations and dreams, but I had never imagined such an embrace and inner peace like this. Thanks be to God for His amazing love, endless blessings, and for His continued presence in our lives! I am forever grateful!

The second journal entry I would like to share with you was dated, Saturday, September 5, 2009. I was working that day and decided to spend my lunch break in prayer, spiritual music and meditation. As I closed my eyes, I tried to envision the beautiful flower garden and bright colours surrounding it; which I dreamt about a couple of weeks prior to this journal entry.

In that dream, the colours were so vibrant and the flowers were absolutely amazing. As I looked around me, I noticed I was the only one there at the time. I felt complete peace and was in awe of my whole surroundings. When I woke up in the morning, I felt fabulous. I again thought about the dream later in the day and I was shocked that I didn't feel afraid or anxious at all in the dream when I noticed I was alone. For many years, I experienced high anxiety when thoughts about being "alone" came to mind. Yet, in this dream, I was at peace and in awe of the beauty that surrounded me.

I believe God was presenting me with a small taste of heaven; confirming to me that heaven truly does exist and how serene and beautiful it is. I also believe God was confirming that I am not and never will be alone, and for me to enjoy the abundant peace that manifests in our lives when we believe and trust in Him. Everything surrounding me was so healthy and vibrant in the dream that it almost glowed. It was so beautiful that I could not even put it all into words.

As I reflected on it today (September 5, 2009), the words "Believe and you will receive" came in my thoughts. I believe God was providing reassurance and encouragement for trust and faith in the days to come. I also feel that this was a message from God for me to let go of my fear of dying. If I put my complete trust and faith in Him, there is absolutely nothing to fear.

As I continued to reflect on God and His love for me, I played some songs of worship that I had put on my mp3 player a few months before. At this very time, the song "Thankful" by Josh Groban started to play. It confirmed much of what I was experiencing at that very moment.

I agree that we truly do have so much to be thankful for in our lives. What powerful words as you listen to his song lyrics! As I continued to listen to the lyrics, I was reminded of the scripture Hebrews 11:1 (NIV) which tells us, *"Now faith is confidence in what we hope for and assurance about what we do not see."*

I believe this song was perfectly timed. It came right in line with the message I received today during reflection, "Believe and you will receive". This also tied right in with the dream I had about the beautiful flower garden. I believe God's message was relayed to me in this way so I could clearly understand His message; to continue believing with unwavering faith in His abilities and promises for us as believers in Christ. I give thanks to God for providing such clarity and reassurance and for helping to strengthen and encourage me along my spiritual journey.

$\mathcal{C}$HAPTER 9

THE POWER OF PRAYER

Ultimately, the power of prayer resides in our God in whom we are praying to. We are told in Philippians 4:6-7 (NLT), *"Don't worry about anything; instead, pray about everything. Tell God what you need, and thank him for all he has done. Then you will experience God's peace, which exceeds anything we can understand. His peace will guard your hearts and minds as you live in Christ Jesus."*

As we continue to read scriptures throughout the Bible, we come to see how God answers prayers that are in agreement with His will. God's answers are not always going to be yes, but they are always going to result in our best interest. When our intentions and requests line up with God's will, and when we continue to pray passionately and diligently, we can then see how powerful God's response will be.

It is therefore so important to teach children early on in life how important it is to pray and give praise to God for all He blesses us with. We also need to explain that God's answer will not always be what they are expecting Him to do, but God's answer will always have the child's best interest at hand. As they continue to grow in faith and trust in God as they mature, they will come to understand God's purposes and reasons for answering their prayers in the way He did. The same holds true for all believers as they mature in their relationship and trusting faith with God our Father and in Jesus Christ.

I find it remarkable when children share their prayers with us. I believe we can all be inspired by their trust and passion in praying to God. My niece Hannah's grade three class was asked to write a prayer that could be read over the intercom at their school. Hannah's prayer was chosen from among her classmates. In knowing that she had written this prayer all by herself at the age of eight, I was so touched and inspired by her words and wanted to share them with you.

As written by Hannah:

Prayer

In the name of the father the son the holy spirit amen.
Dear God,

I love you and praise you each day. My heart beat sings a song of your love. You are the one to trust, you are the one to look up to for help. If I get hurt, fall down, or I'm sad. I can trust you to help me and help others. You are like a team that is working together all the time. You don't only read my mind you read my heart I love you God.

Amen. _Hannah 2002_

By trusting in God's presence to be with me and guide me when I left an abusive marriage and resided in a safety shelter for women, I was able to focused my attention away from the negative circumstances surrounding me onto poetry writing which was very therapeutic for me.

Poetry writing has always been a great way for me to express my innermost thoughts and feelings and serves as a great way for me to journalize my life journey. As I would read back on them, I was amazed on how I could be so strong in faith, even though I felt that I was so vulnerable and weak.

The following poem was written while I was at the safety shelter, reflecting on God's ongoing presence in my life.

Live For Today - Believe In Tomorrow

For guidance and strength I pray,
That my Guardian Angel will light the way,
So I can stay focused on each moment,
And feel protected throughout each day.

When times are tough and challenging,
We must always remember one thing,
For whatever's too heavy to carry,
Our Angel will lend a wing.

Today I lay myself down to sleep,
With a love and trust that I hold deep,
In knowing at no time am I alone,
I can put away my fears and do not weep.

I believe tomorrow I'll be stronger,
And the pain I felt will be no longer,
Knowing my angel is by my side,
I can live for today and each day after.

~

Psalm 91:11 (NLT) tells us, *"For he will order his angels to protect you wherever you go."* With this in mind, I was able to turn my focus away from the uncertainty of how my ex-husband may react once I left the safety shelter, onto trusting God and His heavenly angels for protection.

This poetic prayer to God, conveys my trusting faith in God's miraculous ways of strengthening, enlightening and comforting us by having His angels watching over us and relaying His message to us.

As we see in scripture, the inner peace and special guidance obtained through the angels of God is a blessing from God himself, not through the power of angels on their own. It is through His orders that angels have power to assist us in our lives.

Psalm 91:9-11 (NLT), *If you make the Lord your refuge, if you make the Most High your shelter, no evil will conquer you; no plague will come near your home. For he will order his angels to protect you wherever you go."*

Ultimately, we cannot bear these difficult or traumatic times in our life on our own. It takes a compassionate, forgiving, faithful and loving God to get us through these times.

It is always easy to love and trust God when we have an awesome job, amazing house, secured finances, or when we are in great health. It doesn't take much faith to follow God at the best of times in our lives, but when terminal illnesses or diseases come, or you lose your home or job, or perhaps a loved one dies, we then come to the point where we know we can only depend on God to get us out of the situations we are in.

I came to this realization when I experienced feelings of being at an all-time low in my life wondering where I would turn next, or how I could ever get out of the situation I was in. Once again I put my total trust in God.

Even though I experienced two failed marriages, a car accident, the loss of my mother, grandfather, niece and my cousin and best friend (Mary Anne), I trusted that God would turn things around and still felt that He had great things in store for my life. I knew I just needed to continue to pray and be patient in His blessings for my life.

We need to be open to recognize the signs of God's love and presence during difficult times and know that we are not alone, he is there to carry us.

God continues to strengthen me, enlighten me, and bless me beyond anything I could ever imagine. I continue to believe that our end reward and special blessings from God in our life makes everything worth the risks, challenges, battles and traumas that we may face in our lifetime.

In reading through the Bible, I acquired greater insight into God's desires for our lives. He desires to bless and protect us, to educate and strengthen us, and to guide and deliver us. With this in mind, I have been enlightened and encouraged to hold strong and trust in the power of prayer, trust in God's desire to communicate with us and trust in God's love, power and faithfulness to complete all the good work that He began in each of us.

Our words are very powerful. Sometimes we speak, not being aware that the very thing we say out of our mouths could cause negative situations to occur in our lives or in the lives of others. If we continue to think and speak negatively about our health, our finances, or situations going on in our life or in the life of our family or friends, that is what we can expect to materialize.

"Do not let any unwholesome talk come out of your mouths, but only what is helpful for building others up according to their needs, that it may benefit those who listen." Ephesians 4:29 (NIV)

The words that come out of our mouth are an indication of what is in our heart. Therefore, we need to speak positive words and trust that God will fulfil what we have prayed and voiced into existence for our life and in the lives of others. In this way, we can be a sign to others of the love of God that is within us and bless someone's life that God placed upon us to do in reverence of Him.

With a clean heart and mind and the right spirit within us, we can call on the name of Jesus Christ and trust in the power that is available to us as believers in Jesus Christ as Our Lord, Our Healer, Our Saviour and Our faithful friend, whose amazing love and tremendous blessings are endless.

In times of illness, I continue to find great peace and strength from trusting in the power of prayer and in God's endless abilities in bringing great restoration and blessings in my life and in the life's of those I am diligently praying for. I am a witness to His miraculous healing and will continue to testify of His love and His Greatness!!!

Psalm 30:2 (NIV) says, *"LORD my God, I called to you for help, and you healed me."*

Here is an example of a healing prayer you can pray for yourself or you can substitute the name of the person you are praying for.

Dear Lord, It is you I turn to for refuge, strength, courage, peace and help in times of need. I ask you now Dear Lord, for your continued presence during my illness. Please send your Holy Spirit to remove all doubt, fear and anxiety so I will be at peace while I await your intervention, your miraculous healing and full restoration of my body. In Jesus' Name I pray. Amen.

Jacob, Moses, Abraham, Joseph and many others held strong in faith to God's Word and promises. We see in scriptures how they were strengthened in the midst of their enemies and difficult situations throughout their lives. Go blessed them and their generations favourably because of their unwavering faith and trust in Him and His Word.

As a believer and child of God, we are also descendants of Abraham and God will fulfil His promises as spoken in His Word. We too shall have eternal happiness and heavenly rewards as God promised to fulfil in His covenant with Abraham.

Psalm 105:7-9 (NIV), *"He is the LORD our God; his judgments are in all the earth. He remembers his covenant forever, the promise he made, for a thousand generations, the covenant he made with Abraham, the oath he swore to Isaac."*

What a tremendous gift, awesome love and faithful God we serve!!!

We need to stay in constant prayer and seek direction from God. We cannot have doubt in His promises or His power by taking control back from God to try and make things happen on our own. Only with God are all things possible!

As I continue to pray, worship and glorify God, I trust He will empower me with all I need to serve Him best.

My passion is to follow in Christ's footsteps to help and serve others and to be an example of God's love for my generation and generations to come. Things of this life - people, careers and possessions will pass away, but God's Word and promises are everlasting.

Our spiritual eyes need to be always open and aware of our surroundings and we need to pray for wisdom, guidance and discernment so we can stay on the right path that will lead us into eternal life.

I truly feel that I have obtained so much more throughout my spiritual journey than I ever have, or ever could have, through material possessions. God's blessings have always provided for my needs mentally, physically, financially and spiritually. I am forever grateful and I pray for God's blessings upon each and every one of your lives, in Jesus' Holy Name. Amen!

CHAPTER 10

PRAY FOR THE LOST

I pray for those who have lost their way and for those who, as of yet, have not experienced such a divine love as shown to us by God and by Jesus Christ. Scripture tells us that we are to diligently pray for all people to follow in the ways of our Lord God and for them to be saved as promised to all believers as stated in Scripture.

"I urge, then, first of all, that petitions, prayers, intercession and thanksgiving be made for all people— for kings and all those in authority, that we may live peaceful and quiet lives in all godliness and holiness. This is good, and pleases God our Savior, who wants all people to be saved and to come to a knowledge of the truth." 1 Timothy 2:1-4 (NIV)

As believers and knowing Christ's purpose here on earth, we know *"God sent his Son into the world not to judge the world, but to save the world through him."* John 3:17 (NLT)

Luke 19:10 (NIV) tells us, *"For the Son of Man came to seek and to save the lost."*

During self-reflection and meditation, I recalled a time in my life where I had put other priorities and circumstances ahead of my relationship with God. By steering off my spiritual path, I got lost.

I never lost my true faith in God, but by not keeping God first in my life above all else, I was not able to grow spiritually as God needed me to, or where I needed to be. God gives us the tools we need to grow spiritually, but if we are not willing or able to accept His help or plans at the time, then it will not happen.

God desires that we as Christians, purpose our lives in seeking out the lost and bringing them to God; just as Jesus Christ came into the world to save the lost.

We can assist the lost by educating them on the life, love and teachings of Jesus Christ as expressed in great detail through His precious Word. We can also pray and ask God to open the eyes and ears of the lost, so they may see their need for forgiveness and salvation. I continue to pray for a renewing of the heart and mind of the lost, so they are receptive to the leading of the Holy Spirit in their lives.

God is a loving, patient and forgiving God. He desires for His children to come back to Him. If we repent of our sins and open ourselves up to God's plans for our life, we will continue to grow spiritually and build a deeper relationship with Him. God will continue to guide our steps along our journey and strengthen our faith and trust in Him and in His Word.

I am forever grateful to my friend Pam who introduced me to a Christian Church in 2006. I have grown to great new heights spiritually and obtained tremendous insight and understanding of God's desire for our lives. I was also enlightened to the power we have as believers in the Name and in the Blood of Jesus Christ.

For healing, protection, miraculous works and blessings to manifest in our lives, and in the lives of those we are praying for, we need to apply the Name and Blood of Jesus Christ over our petitions. For example, I ask for the healing blood of Jesus within and over all children, protecting them from illness and harm, in Jesus' Name. Amen!

I believe it is up to us as believers to shine the light of Christ into the lives of others so they too can experience a much deeper and rewarding relationship with Him. It is also an awesome way to shed light in the midst of the darkness around us.

There are many resistant people in this world but as believers we need to try and share of our knowledge and experiences with them. When they have full knowledge of Jesus Christ and how He gave of His life for us and they accept him as their Lord and Saviour, they too can look forward to eternal rewards as promised to all faithful believers.

The Bible tells us how we can get in right standing with God.

"For Moses writes that the law's way of making a person right with God requires obedience to all of its commands. But faith's way of getting right with God says, "Don't say in your heart, 'Who will go up to heaven' (to bring Christ down to earth). And don't say, 'Who will go down to the place of the dead' (to bring Christ back to life again)." In fact, it says, "The message is very close at hand; it is on your lips and in your heart." And that message is the very message about faith that we preach: If you confess with your mouth that Jesus is Lord and believe in your heart that God raised him from the dead, you will be saved. For it is by believing in your heart that you are made right with God, and it is by confessing with your mouth that you are saved." (Romans 10:5-10 NLT)

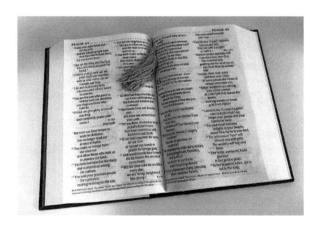

By bringing God's Word into the lives of others, we exemplify the love of Christ. What a great way to serve and glorify God!

My desire in life is to live the best Christian life that I can. If I am not able to bring someone into God's presence, I will continue to pray with confidence in God's power and promise to fulfill our prayers, as I hold firm in trusting faith for their salvation and for salvation of all my generations.

"Therefore I tell you, whatever you ask for in prayer, believe that you have received it, and it will be yours." (Mark 11:24 NIV)

We are not to give up hope or trust in bringing the lost to God. If we earnestly try our best in sharing of our faith and love of God, we never know whose lives we may impact along the way.

Sometimes we may not be able to reach a person for whom we have been trying to shine the light of Christ on, but our efforts will never go unnoticed. We cannot lose trust or faith. God is faithful to complete the good works that began in us. God is always in control!

We are to be patient and forever loving in our efforts as expressed to us in God's Word.

"And we urge you, brothers and sisters, warn those who are idle and disruptive, encourage the disheartened, help the weak, be patient with everyone. Make sure that nobody pays back wrong for wrong, but always strive to do what is good for each other and for everyone else. Rejoice always, pray continually, give thanks in all circumstances; for this is God's will for you in Christ Jesus." (1 Thessalonians 5:14-18 NIV).

God gifts each one of us for the purposes He has destined us to achieve during our lifetime. I believe God desires for me is to share and testify of His Word and His great deeds. By writing this book, I am able to share the power and love of God with many people of various ages, various levels of understanding, and in various parts of the world that I may not be able to reach otherwise.

$\mathscr{C}$HAPTER 11

BELIEVE IN GOD'S PLANS AND PURPOSES FOR YOUR LIFE

I would like to share a new revelation that I wrote in my journal on October 19, 2009.

God is, and will always be, the only one to judge all people and their actions. I made a decision long ago to forgive others as I would like God to forgive me of all my wrong doings.

What I failed to see or understand is that I am to pray for those individuals who are determined to discredit or hurt me and others around them. I prayed for help in learning how to have a divine love of everyone just as Jesus Christ and God Our Father does for us, but until yesterday, I hadn't realized that to obtain a better love of all people, I must forgive them and pray for them.

In dealing with people who repeatedly hurt others with their words and actions at our work place or in our personal lives, we need to forgive these people and ask God for strength and wisdom to rise above the situation at hand.

The new revelation that came to me today is that I have been praying for quite some time now for God to show me what His plan and purpose is for me at my present work place. God knows exactly what I have been going through and why I endured all that I did. I believe that there is something God needed me to do, or still needs me to accomplish, before moving on in my life and in my career.

I realize today that God needed me to be in the midst of all the turmoil at my work place to test my faith and to help me grow stronger in my spiritual walk with Him. Within the past couple of years, I have gained a great deal of patience, which I never had an abundance of before.

I believe God was revealing to me the importance of understanding and totally forgiving who have treated us unjustly. God does not want us to judge, rebel or slander anyone in return. We need to leave the judgement and outcome of their actions in God's hands.

I believe God wanted me to learn how to show unconditional love like He has for us. It is so much easier to love people who respect and love you in return, but I believe God's plan for me was to learn to share a Christian love with everyone.

In an atmosphere surrounded with such negativity and evil words or actions of others, God not only wants us to pray for these people, He wants us to shine His love and light into the hearts and minds of those overshadowed by negative influences in their lives.

"You have heard the law that says, 'Love your neighbor' and hate your enemy. But I say, love your enemies! Pray for those who persecute you! In that way, you will be acting as true children of your Father in heaven. For he gives his sunlight to both the evil and the good, and he sends rain on the just and the unjust alike. If you love only those who love you, what reward is there for that? Even corrupt tax collectors do that much. If you are kind only to your friends, how are you different from anyone else? Even pagans do that. But you are to be perfect, even as your Father in heaven is perfect." Matthew 5:43-48 (NLT)

We as Christians need to ask God to draw these people to Him and pray that they will desire to seek and know Him. We must pray that they will believe in His Word as written in the Scriptures and pray for the Holy Spirit to work within them. We need to ask God to send someone into their lives to lead them to Christ and pray that they will believe in Jesus as their Lord and Saviour. We must also pray that they will turn away from their sinful nature with a desire to walk in the path that God has set out for them.

"There are six things the LORD hates, seven that are detestable to him: haughty eyes, a lying tongue, hands that shed innocent blood, a heart that devises wicked schemes, feet that are quick to rush into evil, a false witness who pours out lies and a person who stirs up conflict in the community." Proverbs 6:16-19 (NIV)

As I wrote this in my journal and focused on what I had written, I believe God needed to bring forth this awareness and understanding of Christ like forgiveness into my heart and mind for which all Christians must live by in their walk with Him.

I truly believe God needed me to see, understand and put what I have learned into practice, so I could move ahead mentally, physically, and spiritually.

God has plans and purposes for each and every one of His children on earth. If we ask Him, He will reveal to us what He has planned for our life and how we can serve Him best in preparation for eternity. With patience and trust, God will not only open new doors for us to walk through, He will also provide us with wisdom, guidance, strength and courage to accomplish goals and responsibilities in our lives.

God blesses each one of us individually with different talents, skills and gifts. He expects us to use these traits to the best of our abilities. He didn't gift us to just benefit our own personal needs. God expects us to serve Him with our gifts and talents by helping others in need.

"Each of you should use whatever gift you have received to serve others, as faithful stewards of God's grace in its various forms." (1 Peter 4:10 NIV)

If uncertainties arise about what you are destined to do according to God's will for your life, take time to pray and meditate and wait patiently for God to answer. He will guide your steps, bless your life and help you to reach your goals.

I thank God for my witty personality and genuine compassion for people. It is a great feeling to be able to brighten someone's day or to provide hope and love for those in need. I am also grateful for my talents in sewing, haircutting and various crafts. This way I am able to help others in need and I can to do so free of charge.

I thank God for this New Revelation and understanding in my life and for teaching me to love as we as Christians are to love with true "Agape Love"; the same type of love that Jesus Christ had for us as expressed in scriptures.

"A new commana I give you: Love one another. As I have loved you, so you must love one another. By this everyone will know that you are my disciples, if you love one another." John 13:34-35 (NIV)

With agape love, we need to commit to striving to be the best we can be no matter how anyone may respond. This true form of love is totally selfless and does not change whether the love given is returned or not.

$\mathcal{C}$HAPTER 12

THE POWER IN
FRIENDSHIPS/RELATIONSHIPS

I personally believe that the most rewarding, most influential and heavenly blessed friendships happen in our lives once we are enlightened to, and understanding of, how important it is to have a special relationship and friendship with God first.

Even knowing the destiny He was facing, Jesus trusted that God was with Him and He remained confident in His Father to take care of the circumstances he was facing. We also need to believe like Jesus, that God is who He says He is, and that God will do what He says He will do.

Once we have a special relationship with God our Father, I believe we will be blessed with special friendships through the people God places in our lives.

Just as my life has been truly blessed with such spiritually uplifting, unconditionally loving and supportive friends, you too can experience such heavenly blessed friendships; beginning with your intimate relationship with God.

To share of my appreciation for two very dear friends – Pam and Linda - I wrote a poem in May of 2009, to express my innermost feelings for our blessed relationship.

<u>My Angel, My Strength, My Friend</u>

In prayers of thanks to God I send,
For gifting my life with you my friend.
Through the light in your eyes and kind words spoken,
My heart opened wide and welcomed you in.

Your wisdom, your honesty and sharing
Has enlightened my soul in seeing
How my life has truly been blessed
With a friendship so special; so heavenly kissed.

God's purpose for all upon this earth
Was uniquely planned before our birth.
I believe His plans for you and me,
Is to share and embrace in all life's beauty.

Your undying faith and compassion speaks loud
And for who you've become, I'm sure He's proud.
Like a golden treasure that no money can buy,
Your angelic ways shine on earth and sky.

~

From the very first day I met Linda, I felt a deep connection with her. She is so genuine and unique in all she believes, speaks and acts. She has blessed my life with such inspiration and encouragement in my spiritual journey since the very beginning of our friendship.

Linda's love for God and trusting faith is clearly seen from all she has overcome, all she continues to do, and in the unconditional love she has for all people. She truly is a great example of Christ-like love in being non-judgmental, by accepting and loving others for whom they are regardless of their appearance, culture, past history or life circumstances.

I believe Linda's character and actions genuinely portray how we are to humble ourselves before God. I know she has truly inspired me.

The importance of being humble is mentioned several times in the Old Testament. During Christ's ministry, He spoke about the importance of being humble. It is also mentioned several times throughout the New Testament in the writings of the Apostles.

For example, Proverbs 11:2 (NIV) tells us, *"When pride comes, then comes disgrace, but with humility comes wisdom."*

And Jesus tells us in Matthew 11:29 (NIV), *"Take my yoke upon you and learn from me, for I am gentle and humble in heart, and you will find rest for your souls."* Jesus is a perfect example for all of us on how we are to live a humble life.

~

Another dear and heavenly blessed friendship I have is with my friend Pam. I met Pam at the long-term care home where I presently working. I had only spoken with her a couple of times when she asked me, "You really do have a hunger and desire to know God better don't you?" And I responded, "Yes, how did you know?" She smiled and asked if I would like to attend a service that was being held at her Christian church.

Being born and raised a different religion, I hesitated at first but then said, "Sure, why not." That very service, March 19, 2006, I remember the Pastor asking us, "If Jesus was before you, asking you to be baptized as an adult as He did, would you do it?" Those very words, and envisioning Jesus Christ before me, I went up and was baptized that very day. My life has changed and has been tremendously blessed from that day on. I have gained tremendous insight and a deeper relationship with Jesus Christ and our Heavenly Father.

I thanked Pam for inviting me to the service, and I thank God for the special spiritual and unconditionally loving friendship I have with her. She has taught me a great deal about Scripture teachings and the importance of keeping God and His Word as my primary focus in life. What a great love and unshakeable trust she has in Our Father God and in Jesus Christ our Saviour. I truly believe that God placed Pam in my life so we could help each other to grow to new heights mentally and spiritually.

Being brought up in a different church from birth, I had strong religious beliefs but I never really knew much about the importance of reading the Bible on a daily basis. We were taught to pray at a very young age but we never read from the Bible. The only time I recall hearing passages read from the bible, was when I was in grade school and when I went to church.

Continuing on in my Christian faith, I read and meditate on God's Word as expressed in the Bible and I have learned so much that I had never known before. It has enhanced my faith and trust in God's Word and in His promises for all of us as believers. I continued to go to this local church and joined in some of their empowerment classes and prayer nights to heighten my relationship with God and with Jesus Christ.

I presently attend another Christian church and trust that God will continue to lead me to wherever he needs me to be along my spiritual journey.

Without God's absolute presence in our lives, and without acquiring a relationship with Him first, who knows what our journey in life would have been like if we followed the paths of the world instead of God's plans and purposes for us?

~

I am forever grateful to God for blessing me once again through the wonderful friendship I experienced with my cousin and best friend, Mary Anne.

I truly admired Mary Anne's unconditional love and acceptance of everyone just the way they were. She had a big heart and open mind about life and friendships. Her words and actions brought so much joy wherever she went. Her great sense of humour helped brighten some of the darkest days in my life.

Mary Anne was so compassionate and caring towards the needs of others around her. She always tried to look at the bright side of things, not letting too much get her down. Mary Anne seemed to rise above negative situations with a stronger spirit and ability to find great happiness in life.

Mary Anne battled cancer and was taken from us in 1989. Her sister and family were forever by her side. For such a very long time I felt extreme guilt because I could not be there for her in her time of need.

At the time of Mary Anne's illness, I was going through major difficulties within my marriage and I was also dealing with bouts of anxiety and panic attacks. I didn't understand why I was feeling so weak and unable to rise above my circumstances. At that time, my relationship with God was not where it is today, and I needed to rely on medication and assistance from the doctor.

I was so overwhelmed with so many fears, questions and uncertainties that I felt guilty because I didn't feel strong enough to be with Mary Anne when she needed me most. I believed in my heart if it was me battling cancer or any other trauma in life, she would have been there for me. This left me with years of feeling guilty because I was unable to be there for her to uplift and encourage her. I truly admire and appreciate the special care and comfort she was able to receive from her loving family who remained by her side.

During an encounter weekend I attended, these thoughts came into my mind once again. I believe God wanted me to face them and to realize that for me to move on in life with great happiness and peace, I needed to let go of the guilt I experienced in not being there for Mary Anne in her time of need and to understand that I was not able to even deal with my own issues during that time. As I reflected on this, I came to realize that I also harboured feelings of blame over my husband for not supporting me with our marital issues and more so with him not being there to help support me during the terminal illness and death of my cousin and best friend.

What God revealed to me that day is that I was so consumed with my own personal issues that I was unable to be by Mary Anne's side during her bout with cancer and that I needed to forgive myself and let go of this guilt.

At the same time, I believe God was telling me to forgive my ex-husband and let go of the blame and negative feelings I felt towards him for not being supportive or present for me in my time of need. I have no idea of what he was feeling or going through at that time either, because he didn't share his thoughts or feelings with me at the time. Because I hadn't forgiven myself, I now understood why I hadn't forgiven my ex-husband for not being there for me as well.

Through God's revealing words in my heart that day, I forgave my ex-husband and also forgave myself and was able to let go of the guilt I once felt. I was then able to let go of these hindrances that could inevitably hold me back from God's blessings. I also experienced tremendous peace in my life and spirit.

I was then able to focus on the special friendship and fond memories I shared with Mary Anne without going into a negative state with feelings of guilt. I thank God for this revelation and new found freedom in my life and thank Him for gifting my life with such a wonderful cousin, a tremendous friend and confidante.

We shared so many terrific memories together. I will always cherish the special days with her and her family. I thank God for the time I did have with her. I was truly inspired by her strong will and desire to stay so positive, loving and happy, regardless of difficult situations that surfaced in her life. Our friendship was so heavenly blessed and absolutely priceless!

The courage and strength seen and felt among the family during their loss, has helped encourage me to continue to hold strong in faith and to never lose sight of the blessings we have been given in life. We never know when someone special to us will be taken away, so we can never afford to take things for granted.

What does God say about friendships? *"Two are better than one, because they have a good return for their labor: If either of them falls down, one can help the other up. But pity anyone who falls and has no one to help them up."* Ecclesiastes 4:9-10 (NIV)

Jesus is the ultimate friend a person could ever have. As stated in the Bible, Jesus says, *"There is no greater love than to lay down one's life for one's friends. You are my friends if you do what I command."* John 15:9-14 (NLT)

There is no other person that has been a greater friend to so many people. Jesus knew his destiny, yet he shed His blood at the cross to redeem us of our sins. He paid the ultimate price for all of us. How great is His Love and unwavering passion to be our friend, our Saviour, our Lord!

True friendship is one of the greatest gifts of life. Whether it be a God favoured, lifetime relationship with a husband or wife that you are praying for, or for special friendships with other like

Christians or God fearing people, we must ask God for His help and blessings that are in line with His plans and purposes for our life. I truly believe that with unwavering trust in God, you too can be blessed favourably with some absolutely amazing friends.

May God bless all of you with heavenly blessed friendships and relationships like He blessed me with! We have an awesome God who desires for us to be happy, healthy and truly blessed. I thank Him for His presence in my life and for His ongoing blessings and guidance in all areas of my life.

$\mathscr{C}$HAPTER 13

BELIEVE IN YOURSELF

As we trust in God and His will for our lives, we will be able to gain confidence in our abilities to be successful in all areas of our lives. We must also be able to love ourselves. Many people struggle with the ability to like themselves or may feel that they are unworthy of love.

Destructive thoughts and feelings of poor self-worth could have come about during childhood years. A teacher, a friend or someone else that we trusted could have instilled these negative and damaging thoughts into our minds.

Regardless how, when or why these thoughts kept us in bondage and stopped us from loving ourselves, it is time to let go of these lies of being unworthy and unlovable.

As the Bible tells us, it is clear that God loves us and created us in His image. God loves us so much that He sacrificed His only Son as proof of His love and to also restore our relationship with God which was abolished by sin.

My heart remains full of love and joy as I hold firm to the truth as expressed in Romans 8:38-39 (NIV) *"For I am convinced that neither death nor life, neither angels nor demons, neither the present nor the future, nor any powers, neither height nor depth, nor anything else in all creation, will be able to separate us from the love of God that is in Christ Jesus our Lord."*

God truly loves us unconditionally. Therefore, we need to embrace this His love and learn to appreciate and love ourselves in the same way.

When negative thoughts about yourself come into your mind, replace them with positive ones. This will become easier and easier the more you practice this positive self-talk and it will also get deep rooted into your spirit. You will then find that you are no longer burdened with self-doubt or humiliation. With ultimate self-confidence you will reach tremendous heights in all areas of your life (mentally, physically, spiritually and financially).

Once we are able to love ourselves, regardless of our imperfections, we can then build and strengthen our God given talents and gifts. If you haven't figured out what talents and gifts you have received from God, you need to discover what they are through trial and error. If you fail at something you thought you were gifted to do, you need to keep searching and trying new things until you become skillful and confident in your abilities.

We must also be open to how God wants to use us, our gifts and our talents. He has a specific and pre-planned vision for each one of us. Are you ready to put aside your fears and excuses in order to fulfill God's purposes for your life? If not today, then when might you be ready?

Ultimate belief and trust in God and in His abilities will bring unshakeable trust and belief in ourselves to accomplish whatever goals we set forth in our lives. We need to believe that with God all things are possible and that God created us to be victorious!

We can choose to be victorious through faith in God, Jesus Christ and the ongoing presence of the Holy Spirit in our lives, or we can choose to follow our own hearts, desires, dreams, and goals.

Are you willing to chance your destiny on your own, or are

you willing to put your total trust in God's hands?

I firmly believe we need to take a leap of faith and trust God and His desires and goals for our life?

Scripture tells us: *"Don't copy the behavior and customs of this world, but let God transform you into a new person by changing the way you think. Then you will learn to know God's will for you, which is good and pleasing and perfect."* Romans 12:2 (NLT)

Hebrews 11:6-11 (NIV) tells us, *"…without faith it is impossible to please God, because anyone who comes to him must believe that he exists and that he rewards those who earnestly seek him. By faith Noah, when warned about things not yet seen, in holy fear built an ark to save his family. By his faith he condemned the world and became heir of the righteousness that is in keeping with faith. By faith Abraham, when called to go to a place he would later receive as his inheritance, obeyed and went, even though he did not know where he was going. By faith he made his home in the promised land like a stranger in a foreign country; he lived in tents, as did Isaac and Jacob, who were heirs with him of the same promise. For he was looking forward to the city with foundations, whose architect and builder is God. And by faith even Sarah, who was past childbearing age, was enabled to bear children because she considered him faithful who had made the promise."*

I would like to share with you how my faith helped me to believe and trust in God, believe in myself, and to gain confidence in being able to overcome traumatic events in my life.

My mother passed away in a car accident that she and I were

in on December 17, 1979. In that same year, my grandfather passed away on April 30th and my niece passed away at three months old on May 3rd. We were grieving three losses in less than eight months.

I know God sent the Holy Spirit to be with us. My father's strength throughout that time was phenomenal. I found so much comfort and strength through Him. Dad's words of encouragement and belief in my abilities and strength of character, provided the courage I needed to rise above these difficult times in my life.

The same holds true for me. I didn't blame God for taking our mother from us, nor did I turn to drugs or alcohol to fill the void that I felt in my life. Even though I was with my mother and driving the car when we got in the car accident, I didn't have feelings of guilt or blame. I didn't feel guilty in thinking the cause of her death was my fault, nor did I blame God for the pain I was experiencing because of our loss. I trusted that things happened the way they did because it was all in God's plans.

I know that I am not the only one who has suffered such great losses. You may have lost a child, sister, brother or dear friend. Our belief in salvation gives us hope that we will once again be reunited in eternity.

I believed God would give me the strength to push forward and rise above the pain and that He would also help me to help others in my family to find peace and understanding. His presence and blessings were truly phenomenal!

I understand that the inner peace I felt was because of the strength, courage and comfort that God blessed me with through the working of the Holy Spirit in my life. I continued to pray to with trusting faith in God. I did not allow myself to be tempted by Satan to turn away from God, or to turn to other destructive substances or ways to find comfort.

From 1990 to 2001 there were two other painful events that took place in my life in which I put total control into God's hands.

I knew with His guidance I could do whatever I needed to do to rise above these situations and to move on in life with encouragement and a peaceful heart. Even though there were periods of fear and uncertainty, I still prayed and trusted in God and trusted that He would provide a way for me to do what would be in my best interest according to His will.

Psalm 34:17-19 (NIV) *"The righteous cry out, and the LORD hears them; he delivers them from all their troubles. The LORD is close to the brokenhearted and saves those who are crushed in spirit. The righteous person may have many troubles, but the LORD delivers him from them all."*

There is no greater strength, courage and peace than that which the Lord Our God can provide. I believe that these life experiences have helped my faith in God grow deeper and stronger and helped to intensify my relationship with Him. I was able to focus on what God had in store for me, rather than the uncertainty of my circumstances.

Throughout our life, I believe our faith will be tested in many ways. By continuing my spiritual walk with God to be the best Christian I can be to serve Him and bless others through my words and actions, I will diligently seek His advice and will for my life. I will not let negative situations or words of unbelievers overshadow my trust and faith in God or His Word. I will continue to cover myself with the full armor of God to fight and win the good fight of faith as told to us in Scripture.

"Therefore, put on every piece of God's armor so you will be able to resist the enemy in the time of evil. Then after the battle you will still be standing firm. Stand your ground, putting on the belt of truth and the body armor of God's righteousness. For shoes, put on the peace that comes from the Good News so that you will be fully prepared. In addition to all of these, hold up the shield of faith to stop the fiery arrows of the devil. Put on salvation as your helmet, and take the sword of the Spirit, which is the word of God. Pray in the Spirit at all times and on every occasion. Stay alert and be persistent in your prayers for all believers everywhere." Ephesians 6:13-18 (NLT)

I would like to share another journal entry which was dated September 4, 2009. My friend Linda came into work and gave me a quote that she had found in the newspaper. Linda told me that when she read it, she automatically thought of me. I researched the article she gave me and found that Kent M. Keith was the author. It was known as the Paradoxical Commandments and was written by Kent in 1968.

Linda shared her thoughts and feelings with me. She explained how inspired she was in seeing that regardless of the challenges and struggles I faced in my life, I continued to rise above difficult situations and never lost hope or faith in God and continued on with great strength and courage.

Linda also shared how she was inspired in witnessing how I continue to give of myself and my ability to forgive others in spite of the ongoing challenges surrounding me. Her shared words were so heartwarming and truly enlightening. I believe God was telling me (through Linda and her comforting words) to continue to be happy; continue to grow; and continue to forgive.

I believe we are indeed to be the best we can be (as Christians after God's heart). I will continue to share of my testimonies, my life experiences and my spiritual journey with others, in hopes that they too can experience such a divine love, exceptional peace, and everlasting happiness from this life into eternity.

You too can share of your testimonies and spiritual journey with others by journaling your progress throughout the days, months and years.

You can also honour and glorify God by sharing your experiences with other people from your Church, work place or community. As you begin documenting your thoughts, feelings and experiences, it will bring about great awareness and understanding of where you started out in life, how far you have come and where you are headed.

Journaling helps to focus more intensely on what is in our heart and mind. It can bring great peace, hope and joy in our life and into the lives of others we share our journey with.

CHAPTER 14

GOD'S MIRACULOUS SIGNS AND WONDERS

God continues to communicate His love, desires and guidance for all His children through prayer and meditation, spiritual music and books, or even through various media. God also reveals great things through pastors, church leaders and those whom He places in our lives to help educate and assist us in achieving our divine purposes and destiny.

When we take time to look at what's going on in the world, our lives, or in the lives of family and friends, we can see that God is still doing amazing miracles, signs, and wonders all around the world.

A sign of God's awesomeness can be seen in every heart that is healed from fear, anxiety, depression, pain or suffering and by every individual who has been cured from life threatening illness and disease.

Too many people look at the devastating events around the world and blame God for what took place. A true test of faith is when we can look at these traumatic events going on around us and we turn to God and trust that He will help us, heal us, or comfort us in our times of need, and not turn away from Him and blame Him for all life's misfortunes.

Although we don't understand why certain events occur in life, with prayer and diligence in seeking God for wisdom and revelation we are able to obtain greater insight and understanding.

God's wonders can be seen all around us. Through His creation of earth, water, sky and every living thing, we get a little glimpse of God's wisdom and power. We see in Scripture that through His spoken words everything came into existence.

"The Lord merely spoke, and the heavens were created. He breathed the word, and all the stars were born. He assigned the sea its boundaries and locked the oceans in vast reservoirs. Let the whole world fear the Lord, and let everyone stand in awe of him. For when he spoke, the world began! It appeared at his command." Psalm 33:6-9 (NLT)

Even in the toughest of times we need to thank God for all His many blessings in our lives and thank Him for what He is about to do in the coming days, months and years on our behalf.

With total trust in God and His miraculous powers, we too can be blessed with a miracle in our lives. I can attest to that by one of my own life experiences and by God's miraculous healing power that I have witnessed in the lives of others around me.

I have mentioned earlier on in my book how my mother and I were in a car accident in December of 1979. When I looked back at how tremendously damaged the car was, it is hard to believe that there were any survivors. Due to the impact of the accident, I had passed out for a short time. When I came to, I remember looking at my mother who was unresponsive and telling her that I was going to get us out of the car and get help. Even though we were trapped in the car by a ditch on both sides I found amazing strength to be able to force my side of the car door open at least a couple of inches so the men at the scene could pry it open enough for me to get out.

I remember to this day, sitting in the ambulance with the two attendants and my brother Mike and I heard another dispatcher saying that the other victim's vitals were weak. I calmly looked at the two attendants and my brother Mike at the time and said, "Her vitals are weak for a reason, it is her time to go." They looked at me as though they were shocked by my comments.

I just had an overwhelming feeling that regardless how hard they were trying to get her out of the car to help her, I believed in my heart that her death was destined to be that day. God has a set time and day for everything to take place in each of our lives, from the time He formed us in our mother's womb up until our death.

Even though I was experiencing tremendous shock and great sadness over the accident and death of my mother, I also had an extraordinary acceptance that it was God's will for her that day. The unbelievable strength, courage and comfort I had at the scene of the accident and the days following, I know were through the miraculous works of God Our Father. My mother had passed away that day but I miraculously only had a bruised kidney, no broken bones or life threatening injuries.

God's miracle for my life that day not only kept me safe, but it helped me gain great faith and trust in Him, and He provided tremendous emotional and physical strength and healing in my life during one of the times I needed Him most. What an awesome sign that God is true to His word. He never leaves us in our time of need and He continues to perform miracles in so many lives.

My sister Lisa at nine years old was sitting on my father's lap and said, "Dad I know God wanted Mom today, but I am glad He left us Karen."

As expressed through the words and perception of my sister, I believe the Holy Spirit was working within her to provide wisdom and understanding. Even at such a young age, she accepted that my mother's passing was God's will, but she didn't blame God for what happened. Instead she thanked God for His blessing; her sister's life was saved and miraculously unharmed.

What a tremendous gift and miracle that took place in my life and I give ultimate thanks to God. I believe God has plans and purposes to further complete in my life. As long as I live, I will continue to testify of His love, power and presence in my life and the lives of others. Our God truly is an awesome God!!!

I believe God unites and/or reunites us with the people he destines to be in our lives; whether it be for a specific reason, a season or a lifetime. For example, God blessed my life with a heartwarming and high spirited reunion with my cousin Debbie.

Debbie and Rob

Debbie lived only one block away from my house since we were young children and I have such fond memories of our life throughout the years. During high school years, Debbie met a wonderful man named Rob, whom she later married. We didn't keep in contact much she and her husband began their new life together and I moved out of my family's home to begin a new chapter in my life as well.

I believe a God planned intervention brought us back together with a greater plan and purpose for our lives. With Debbie's permission, I would like to share how God performed miraculous healing in her life.

In July of 2009, Debbie had gone for a couple of tests on her lungs and the doctor told her that she was to have immediate surgery to remove one-third of one of her lungs. This section was sent away for examination of the diseased tissue. The results came back inconclusive so they had to be sent away for further testing.

My brother called to tell me about Debbie and her surgery. I told him that I would go see her and offer assistance with anything she may need. When I reached her home, uncertain of what to expect, I was a little nervous as to what I would say. I erased all thoughts from my head and trusted that the Holy Spirit would guide my thoughts, words and actions.

So many times we rehearse over and over again as to what we will say, instead of allowing the Holy Spirit to guide us. For me, I continue to give control to the Holy Spirit who has never let me down.

I found Debbie to be in great spirits, never once complaining about anything. I told her that if she needed me in any way I would be more than happy to be there for her. I also told her that we needed to continue believing in the power of prayer and trust in God's healing of the sick and His miraculous powers.

I also told Debbie that our Church was holding a world day of prayer service and that I was bringing her intentions forward in prayer. I believed with trust and faith in God that regardless of the outcome of the test results, God was going to guide us every step of the way. Debbie never once lost hope or faith. She truly inspired me and her family beyond words.

While we were awaiting her results, Debbie shared with me how she is a cancer survivor and had been diagnosed with breast cancer eight years prior to her lung surgery. She had lumpectomy surgery at that time, followed by 18 rounds of radiation. Debbie never told anybody other than her husband, her brother and sister. She never wanted her mother to find out about her illness because she didn't want her mother to worry. God miraculously healed Debbie from breast cancer and she trusted God would be forever present throughout her life.

Debbie's mother also had breast cancer when she was 36 years old and had to undergo a mastectomy, radiation and chemotherapy treatments. Her mother miraculously was a cancer survivor and held firm in her faith in God as well. Her mother passed away at 70 years old from a heart condition. God miraculously healed her mother from cancer and she was blessed with another 34 years being cancer free. Our God is truly an awesome and healing God!

Knowing that Debbie's father had passed away a few years ago from lung cancer, of course questions came to mind as to whether she too would have lung cancer as many think about from generation to generation. But I know God is a healing God and through prayer and faith in Him, we can break the generational cycle of illness and misfortune over someone's life.

I prayed diligently and called a few friends to ask them to keep Debbie in their prayers as well. Debbie soon called me with the results of her tests. She excitedly told me, "It's not cancer!" How relieved and tremendously grateful I am that God chose to bless her life with a miracle once again.

God's miraculous works that took place in Debbie's life not only blessed her and her family, it also inspired me and helped me to gain an unshakeable trust in the power of God Our Father. What a great testimony of how belief and trust in God can provide miraculous outcomes and great rewards.

If we want God to do positive and amazing things in our life, we need to think positive and not get distracted by negative thinking or doubts about His abilities to change things around.

I wanted to share these life experiences with you in the hope that you too may be inspired and encouraged by the wonderful signs, wonders and miracles of God our Father. He is still alive and active in our lives even today, just as He promised to never leave us.

I also pray for all of you to experience God's unfailing love and ongoing presence in your lives so you too can be blessed beyond your wildest imaginations here on earth and in the heavenly rewards awaiting them as faithful believers. In Jesus' Holy Name I pray, Amen!

I would like to share a special poem that I wrote for Debbie in March 2011.

<u>So Heavenly Blessed</u>

What a great inspiration you are Debbie
In expressing a love so unconditionally
With a high spirited and unshakeable bond
God gifted this friendship between you and me.

In receiving a diagnosis so chilling
That for many would be overwhelming
With utmost faith and courage
You trusted in God's power and healing.

Your wisdom and spiritual insight
Emanates such a tremendous light
And Jesus' love that radiates through you
Is clearly seen in your eyes so bright.

Without doubt or hesitation
I believe our renewed connection
That is so heavenly blessed
Was definitely by God's intervention.

My words only in part can express
My true appreciation and thankfulness
So let my prayers and my actions
Be forever blessing and endless.

~

Unknown to me at the time, Debbie had also written a poem for me in that same year. Her poem truly touched my heart and she continues to be a blessing in my life. It is such a rewarding feeling to know how someone else can be inspired by our words and actions and that they too desire a deeper relationship with God.

I heard of the saying, "two hearts beating as one", referring to couples in love sharing the same interests and finishing each other sentences, etc., but now, I also believe in "two minds thinking as one."

The more and more Debbie and I are together, the more I see "our minds thinking as one"; as seen in the beautiful poem she wrote for me below.

God's Messenger of Love, Friendship and Commitment

We laughed, we cried and when I am troubled I think of her.
We are family and as children we played in innocence and wonder.
Connected later in life as if no time has passed us by,
There should be no reason to question why.

She has helped me see the world in a different way,
Her love and inspiration is a common stay.
God and his love has been her journey,
To understand this and learn from her is key.

There are not many people that you can clearly trust.
Staying close, even if it is just a moment in a day is a must.
To not do so would dishonour our connection
Which God has brought together with conviction.

Not many people one can say is truly your friend,
To share dreams, hopes and fears to no end.
As we continue to grow old and experience more moments,
Our next chapter will bring comfort, excitement and truly a sense

Of where we are and where we are supposed to be,
Through God's generosity and glorious beauty,
The world and my life is a better place
With a lady that handles challenges with such grace.

Written with love for Karen,
D.M. March 2011

$\mathscr{C}$HAPTER 15

IN WORDS OF THANKS

Our military men and women give unselfishly of their lives for their country and for freedom, not knowing what the day or tomorrow may bring. In words of thanks, I wrote the following poem, which is dedicated to of each and every one of them.

Our Military Heroes

In a war led by greed, power, or national conflict
And a world filled with true uncertainty,
If not for our men, our women, our heroes,
Who knows where our lives would be.

Strengthened by the hands of God
And the hearts of their family,
They give of themselves so unconditionally
For all world peace and unity.

We can show our love and support
Through the power of prayer,
So they can be guided and protected
When things seem too hard to bear.

There are not enough words
That could deeply express
Our heartfelt thanks and appreciation
For their gift of unselfishness.

(K.A.D. 2004)

~

The Bible tells us in John 15:13 (NLT), *"There is no greater love than to lay down one's life for one's friends."* How blessed we are, because of their love for us and our country.

This scripture also reminds us of the amazing love of Christ. Jesus loved us so much that He sacrificed His life to free us from sin and death, even though He knew He was going to be persecuted and crucified. Jesus stood firm in obedience and trusting faith to fulfill God's purpose for His life on this earth. There is no greater love than this!

We need to question ourselves. Are we willing to submit our lives to God? With our voluntary actions in following God, His Word, His commands and His plans and purpose for our life, we

83

can confidently look forward to great rewards for our future and for future generations to come. God promises us heavenly rewards for all eternity.

God is the only one who can safely guide you to reach the goals that He set out for you to seek in your lifetime. The only way to get this ultimate guidance and protection is to submit your life to Him and trust Him to fulfill your needs according to His will.

"Even to your old age and gray hairs I am he, I am he who will sustain you. I have made you and I will carry you; I will sustain you and I will rescue you." Isaiah 46:4 (NIV)

Heaven is for eternity – our earthly life is not! What choices are you willing to make to bring positive rewards into your life and into the lives of others?

In 2002, I wrote this poem giving thanks to God for blessing my life with such wonderful parents and siblings.

Our House, Our Home

For such wonderful parents, I thank God above.
They taught us to live, to respect and to love.
Their continuous teachings of faith and religion
Has taught us forgiveness and to find goodness within.
Our House, our home, our lives and dreams
Has truly grown stronger each year it seems.
For you Pat and Lisa, Mike, Doug and Len,
Special thanks and prayers to God I send.
I will cherish the memories of days with my family
And pray for those people less fortunate than me.

My brothers and sisters have been truly supportive in all my endeavors. They have always been by my side when I needed them most. They provided great comfort and understanding during my bouts of anxiety and panic attacks. I am truly grateful for their unconditional love, patience, understanding and encouragement throughout the years. As playmates and then friends, we shared and continue to share such a unique and special bond.

Photos below are of special memories we share as siblings and the fun, love and support we continue to share with nieces and nephews.

I pray that the special bond of unconditional family love and support forever lives on throughout generations to come. In Jesus' Name, Amen!

My heart is full of gratitude for the family God blessed me with. In turn, I desire to glorify and honour God in all I say and do, as an expression of my appreciation and love for who He is, all He has done, and all He continues to do in my life and in the lives of my family and friends.

In words of thanks to my family, I wrote a poem for each one of them in 2004 and gave it to them for Christmas. Below is a poem I wrote for my sister Lisa.

Sister "Lee" Love

One great present from God above
Was through our parents devoted love,
Specially given to our family,
Was a precious baby named Lisa Marie.

Through the years you've been known as "Lee"
And I cherish the memories of you and me.
You've been blessed now as a wife and mother,
With a terrific son and two wonderful daughters.

A sincere love shown to me from you,
Was in knowing just what to say or do.
When I was sick or had anxiety,
You truly understood and were there for me.

One special memory I would say,
Is on each other's Wedding Day
Maid-of-Honour we had been,
As a sister and best friend.

With love to "Lee"
With thanks from me,
Karen - 2004

The following photos are of her and me on my Wedding Day in November of 1999 and me at fourteen years old with my precious baby sister (Lisa).

Special Memories Live On

Nobody could ever fill the void of a loved one who passed on but through God's good graces, a loss or sorrow can be turned around by unexpected blessings.

I was comforted and strengthened while grieving the loss of my mother. I truly believe the healing and peace I experienced was because of the Holy Spirit working within me.

Although we may not understand God's reasoning's for how, why or when He takes a loved one, we can be rest assured that God has a plan, a purpose and set time schedule for all things to take place in our lives.

I believe God provides us with the tools we need to complete all things we are destined to do. In time, God's time, we will have answers to our many questions. We must continue to rely on God, knowing He is in control and that He will provide answers to our prayers and help and comfort us in times of need.

We can be uplifted even during a loss of a dear friend or family members by focusing on all those special moments we shared during their lifetime. We can hold dear to the fact that yes, they were taken from our life, but the special memories will live on in our heart.

My Mother, (Lucille Mailloux Desjardins)

My mother's determination in keeping God as our utmost priority in life has given me a deep rooted trust in my faith, myself and whatever life challenges came my way.

I had moved out of the house when I was 19 and moved back home in January of 1979, just before my 22nd birthday. My mother often wished that I would move back home. I thank God for His intervention and for circumstances that led me to move back home. I had one whole year with my mother before she died in December of that same year.

We were given many gifts that last year of sharing special times and moments that are etched in my memory. She was not just my mother; she became my dear friend and confidante. My mother vowed that she was going to learn to drive, sew and win the jackpot at the bingo hall before she died.

Who knew that she would definitely reach her dreams before she passed? She got her driver's license a couple of years before I moved home in 1979 and she learned to sew in the summer of that year. One week before she passed, she and I won the jackpot at the bingo. She was so very happy and wanted to go out and buy a few more Christmas gifts. It was on that very shopping day that she and I were in a car accident and she passed away.

Even though we were grieving the loss of my mother, I chose to focus on the positive things around us. I told our family how we were fortunate that mom already had bought gifts that she wanted us to have for Christmas so we should celebrate her life and memories, not focus on her death and our loss.

We had lots to celebrate; fond memories, our unconditional love for one another as a family, and our trust that we will one day be reunited with her. I believe this positive thinking once again was because of the presence and working of the Holy Spirit within me.

My father's courage and strength during this time was remarkable. His unwavering faith in God encouraged me to hold strong in prayer and trust in God's plans for our lives. As time went on, I remember sharing with others how I received strength from my dad, yet my dad says he got his strength through me. Without a doubt, I believe our strength came from God through the presence of the Holy Spirit in our lives.

Blessings Of A Father's Love

I have utmost love and respect for my father. He always provides encouragement, understanding, wisdom and compassion. Whether it was a kiss, hug or shoulder to cry on, he always seemed to know how to make things better. Together we laughed and cried and shared our feelings from deep inside. Dad's caring and open mind allowed us to trust and confide in him.

I will always treasure the many fond memories from our childhood. Dad made time to play with us, read to us, take us to the park and even patiently help us with our homework. He was not just our dad, he was also a father figure to other kids who didn't have a father present or active in their lives. Dad always had more than enough love to go around!

When I look back on this now, I do not recall any one of my family members being upset when dad shared his attention with other kids. To this day, there are still a couple of my sister's friends that still refer to him as "Dad".

My father has a great sense of humor. I guess I am a "chip off the old block" as the saying goes. I am forever grateful for having a father who was also my advisor, protector and provider. He has always been a great provider spiritually, mentally, physically and financially. What an awesome father and best friend! I believe God truly blessed our family with the best of father's here on earth.

~

More Than an M.D.

Another amazing blessing in my life came about through the words of wisdom and phenomenal medical care from a former doctor of mine; which I will refer to as Dr. Mick G.

I was introduced to Dr. Mick G. through an Aunt of mine. I mentioned to my Aunt how I felt that I was in need of professional counseling to deal with some anxiety issues I was facing at the time. My Aunt explained how compassionate, understanding and helpful her family doctor had been in her life and suggested for me to see him. She explained how the doctor was still taking on new patients. I immediately booked an appointment with him. What an awesome referral I received!

Dr. Mick G.'s professionalism, shared personal experiences, and passionate heart in helping others medically and psychologically, was a true blessing in my life. He explained how he was able to overcome some of the very same experiences that I shared with him.

He was a great listener and wise counselor. Dr. Mick G. had eventually become a loyal and trusted friend, not just my family doctor. I believe his care, compassion and sincere passion to bring healing and optimum results for each and every one of his patients, both mentally and physically, was an essential part of his purpose on earth destined by God.

Dr. Mick G. had some health issues of his own that he was also dealing with, but he never let it get him down or distracted. It seemed like his passion was definitely greater than his ailments.

God knew exactly what I needed in my life at that very time. I thank God for the wonderful care and healing Dr. Mick G. was able to provide in my life and in the lives of many of his patients. I could never begin to explain in great detail how he absolutely blessed my life.

It is so amazing to see how God works through a variety of people, a variety of professions and in a variety of ways. Once we hold firm in trusting faith we can all experience such a profound love of God as He continues to provide for our every need.

Dr. Mick G. passed away approximately 15 years ago, but his words of wisdom forever live on in my heart. Through the help and encouragement I received from Dr. Mick G., I am able to help encourage others in some of their personal struggles as well. I believe one of the reasons why we are presented with some difficult situations in our lives is because God wants to test us our faith, so we in turn can help others in similar situations.

A Precious Gift

I always loved to be around children since I began babysitting at 11 years old. Their love and energy has always been an uplift and blessing in my life. So many children are wise beyond their years. In 2004 I wrote the poem below, giving thanks and recognition to God for blessing our lives with such a precious gift.

Through A Child's Eyes

Children often see life
As so pleasant and pure,
While others view life
As one huge adventure.

They know not what
Tomorrow will bring
And don't waste time
On fears or worrying.

Your patience and support
To listen and praise
Will strengthen hopes and dreams
Through challenging days.

Their unique little talents
And endless hours of energy
Provides happiness and inspiration,
God's gift to you and me.

Throughout my book, I mention just a few people who touched my life in countless ways, but I also give thanks to God for all of you.! I am sincerely grateful for the relatives, friends and others God has blessed my life with, as well as, those I have yet to meet through God's divine intervention.

There will be all kinds of people who come in and out of our lives. We can be impacted by many people and in many ways than we could ever know or imagine. In turn, we too can impact the lives of other's more than we can even begin to fathom.

God continues to place spiritually uplifting and loving friends in my life. They have helped me to grow in my spiritual journey with such a comforting and inspiring outlook on how I face life and its many challenges.

I also thank God for all I have gone through in my life, the good and the bad. It has helped me to become the person I am today. I have NO regrets! When one door closed in my life, God opened another. I believe everything that occurred was because of God's blessings or a lesson to be learned to strengthen my faith and trust in God, in Jesus Christ and the Holy Spirit.

One important thing to remember along our life journey is the truth that:

ABOUT THE AUTHOR

Karen Anne Desjardins, was born and raised in Windsor, Ontario, Canada. She is passionate about seeing individuals deepen their relationship with God.

In her hunger to serve and honour God, Karen's heart was led to share of God's tremendous love, His many blessings and promises for all believers (as expressed in His Word). Her passion to exemplify the love of Christ, led to the writing of this inspiring and captivating memoir.

By sharing her spiritual journey, Karen hopes to inspire others who may have lost their way back to God and to help those who as of yet, have not experienced such an intense love acquired through a personal relationship with God.

With a passion to achieve God's plans and purposes for her life, Karen's hunger for spiritual growth and strengthening her relationship with God continues on.

Karen Desjardins
Windsor, Ontario, Canada
email: kdesjardinsb2b@hotmail.com
website: https://b2bfaith.com